Compiled and edited
by
Joy Petit-Gittos

BA (Hons.); MIPPMDip; Dip.Couns; Dip.s.m.cou; MSFTR.

ATHENA PRESS
LONDON

AWAKENING

From
Companion of the Earth

Spoken By
Blue Mountain

Through the Voice Mediumship
of
Reverend Gayna Hilary Petit-Gittos
1989–2002

133
(AWA)

AWAKENING
Copyright © The Blue Mountain Trust Ltd 2008
Cover design © Reverend Gayna Petit-Gittos BA (Hons.) Ill. 2007

7

RS

ISBN 10-digit: 1 84748 055 1
ISBN 13-digit: 978 1 84748 055 2

First Published 2008 by
ATHENA PRESS
Queen's House, 2 Holly Road
Twickenham TW1 4EG
United Kingdom

Printed for Athena Press

This book is dedicated to my twin sister, Gayna.

She has dedicated her life to the work of Blue Mountain and 'Companion of the Earth', enabling them to deliver an ancient wisdom to the people of this world. This wisdom is designed to awaken an individual to the pathway of Spiritual Growth.

ACKNOWLEDGMENTS

I would like to thank my own Spirit Companions (known to me, under a collective title, as 'Council') for providing opportunities in my life, which have allowed me to transcribe (from audio tapes), compile and edit the words of 'Companion of the Earth'.

I would also like to thank the Spirit of my late great grand-mother, Florence, for her patience and kindness during the time that she and I have spent compiling this book together. Without her guiding hand and inspired thoughts, this book would not be in existence.

Finally, I wish to thank Martyn Hunt, Angela Lidgbird, Malde Odedra and Bob Simpson, for their support and encouragement whilst completing the latter stages of this book.

TABLE OF CONTENTS

POEMS

PREFACE

This book consists of a compilation of the numerous individual talks, lectures, demonstrations, seminars and conversations with the Spirit Guide 'Blue Mountain' between 1989 and 2002.

He is the representative of a group of spirit beings who are united under the title 'Companion of the Earth'. He communicates with this world through the remarkable voice mediumship of his eternal soulmate: reverend Gayna Petit-Gittos (affectionately called Tywane).

Blue Mountain has spent a lifetime blending with Gayna's energy frequency. By his own admission, he has not communicated, and will not communicate through any other person. However, he may often communicate with people in this world through dialogue with their own Companions.

For many years, the words of Companion of the Earth have been spoken by Blue Mountain, in Switzerland, America and the United Kingdom. These words are not limited to adults alone; children have also benefited from his wisdom.

The information contained in this book, is a universal philosophy about the eternal cycle of life. Many spirit beings, throughout history, have brought the same message. It is timeless, because it is the truth.

Blue Mountain's words have been carefully preserved during the accumulation, transcription and editing process, so that his personally identifiable character, personality and pattern of speech shine through this book about life.

INTRODUCTION – by Blue Mountain

Many human beings believe, implicitly, that love is associated with your world, but this is not so. It is an energy that is vibrant around your universe, in many dimensions that exist. This vibration of energy links all life together.

Tywane and I are joined together for eternity. We are joined through love. So, when I was requested to help your world and your people, I chose Tywane to return with me. She agreed to help me with the work of 'The Companion'. We have been able to utilise this state of blending our energy together, so, to prevent unnecessary time developing the blending process, we again use this state known to you today.

I will not return to the 'World of Matter' now, because there is work for me to do in many different areas of life, and I am not referring to the life of matter. There is a group of souls to which I belong that is moving in a different area, but I have agreed to come now with my friends from the 'World of Light'. Together, we are 'Companion of the Earth' for the duration of Earth's transition.

Tywane will gain great benefit from the experiences placed before her. Likewise, I, too, gain benefit from the experiences placed before me, and we help each other. Remember, all forms of life helps each other. There will not be just one soul gaining benefit from the obstacles of life.

I have been travelling around your country for several years now. I have been trying to penetrate the very hard surface that has been built around the thinking of the people. Over a long, long time, there has been indoctrination by certain people, in certain areas, so creating difficulty for the opening of the thoughts within the minds of people.

I am here for everyone. My work is to bring knowledge to all people around your world, because your world is changing. The evolution of the planet requires a greater knowledge being brought to your people, but many human beings do not like to release the power and control within their hands, so they place fear within the minds of the people. Very slowly, my people from the World of Light are penetrating this fear.

I have been requested to bring the light of knowledge, truth and reality to your country, your world, where there is the darkness of fear.

There will come a time when all people will be aware of the truth of the World of Spirit, but my people and I have to walk very carefully. The emotions of people are like eggs, if I tread too heavily they will break. So I am very careful, because I care about life (human beings, animals and nature) and I wish only to bring love to all people.

CHAPTER 1

Blue Mountain's Story

Told by Blue Mountain to the writer

Blue Mountain and Gayna (Gay) once lived together on Earth as husband and wife. They were known then as Two Trees and Tywane. In due time, they each passed from this world to the world of Spirit where they were re-united. Following a period of time together, they each went through a deeply private process, which gave them an understanding of the lessons, which they had learned and not learned during their lives on Earth. Then they came together again and were in total peace with each other.

Their environment now changed and the light around them grew. Colours sparkled like fresh water from the spring. The atmosphere around them became very fine and they both felt themselves become lighter. They had now moved to the World of Light. They had a new home in this more refined environment, where they carried out different activities to the ones they had been used to. Gay joined the 'Ladies of Blue Light' and, as a result, achieved the private title of Rose. No longer was she a woman of form and shape; instead, she shone, emanating a blue light, the light of ultimate sensitivity. The Ladies of Blue Light were ladies of the heart and now radiated as pure light. The blue light of Gay had a fine depth and vibration to it. Blue Mountain, too, ceased to have shape and form. Instead, he emanated the white light of power with a hint of the purple of profound understanding. To each other they glowed, and this was a very strange experience for them both.

Very slowly, they learned how to merge their colours together. They spent a long time learning this technique and, as they did so, grew strong together. With others around them, slowly, they all learned how to blend their energy together, and from the heart of the group came the white light of power. This was directed to the Earth and to other worlds also, and continued until the time when the group was requested by the Great Spirit to assist directly with the changes to the 'World of Matter' (the planet Earth).

Blue Mountain had no knowledge of the levels, or realms, of vibrating energy through which he passed, from the time of his arrival into the 'World of Spirit' until the time of mergence. He was predominantly aware of changing structures and of a finer and finer atmosphere very slowly engulfing Gay and himself. When the mergence took place all who were involved became one. In order for Gay to join the Ladies of Blue Light, she had to spend time learning to accustom herself to the power of this group. Blue Mountain joined with the 'Brothers of White Light' and received the title of 'White Cloud'. Then these two groups joined together and the energy of each group blended to became one. Not all women who had progressed with Blue Mountain and Gay joined the 'Ladies of Light'. Some women, who had lived in the form of a woman, when they became colour, joined the body of the White Light.

During the time of mergence there was total peace, total serenity. The power of the white light was engulfing. The strength from all the beings together was the sustenance for the group, and as a group they were able to learn together. They learned of the stars and of the many great realms of faster and faster vibrations of energy. The group began to move as a whole, and the more they learned the further they moved.

Then came the time when the knowledge of the request

permeated throughout the light. When the group knew of the task that had been placed before them, they began to learn how to release themselves in order to become individual again. Once the mergence had taken place, it took time to learn how to become individuals, but the knowledge of mergence remained within the soul of each member of the group.

When they had achieved the reversion of the merging process, then it was time for them, as a group, to map out the process that would achieve their goal. So, they considered for a long time the necessary ingredients required for both the achievement of their objective, and the assistance for Gay during her earthly life. Whilst the group was doing this Gay was choosing her parents. She eventually made her choice from two people in the World of Light. They, in turn, made their choices regarding their own existence. This meant that the preparation period was a long and intricate process, because it would result in quite important changes that would benefit both the World of Matter and the World of Light.

With Blue Mountain and Gay came many of the group to which they belonged. Together, they made preparations for her to go through the chrysalis process that would result in her birth into the World of Matter. To Blue Mountain and his people, Gay was leaving them, and this was a time of deep sadness, because one of their own was departing. The group however, gained their strength from the knowledge that there would come a time when Gay's memory would be opened and stimulated, so creating a bridge between the beautiful World of Light and herself. So Gay began her journey.

At last the day came. A circle of friends, who sat together regularly every week, gathered at the normal time of 7pm. Half an hour later the meditation music was switched on whilst Gayna settled back into her chair, closed her eyes, took a deep breath and relaxed. Within a further half hour a presence had joined them. Under its influence Gayna, her eyes closed, stood up and looked at each person present within the room. It was on this occasion, and to everyone's complete amazement, that her mouth opened and a man's voice spoke the words "I exist; I EXIST." Not one person stirred. He started to speak again, saying, "I am here!" Then, with great dignity, he withdrew from Gayna, allowing her to return to normal. The excitement from the group was unparalleled by any emotion they had ever experienced whilst sitting together. There they sat, five mature, rational people, now on the verge of discovering the reality of the World of Spirit from a man whose name, he would later tell them, was Blue Mountain. When he had last walked upon the earth he had been called Two Trees, the eternal loving companion of Tywane.

It took time for Blue Mountain to learn to speak through Gayna. To begin with he spoke very little, uttering occasional monosyllabic words, which had to be pieced together by members of Gayna's home circle. Gradually his speech improved, and it was noticed how much he enjoyed talking to Gayna's family and friends. During the first year of this development, there were times when some of Blue Mountain's colleagues (from the spirit group called 'Companion of the Earth') who were helping him with his work, would entrance Gayna and bring their own distinct style of presence and voice, which were very different to those of Blue Mountain. Within a year he was able to communicate on a regular basis using full sentences.

Since Blue Mountain first made his presence known to Gayna, many people have witnessed the development of their union together. This development has been like the slow growth of a rose, emitting the fragrant perfume and beautiful colours of appreciation and success, together with the painful experiences associated with all growth; the thorns of anguish and uncertainty. The awakening of his existence set both him and Gayna upon a pathway of service, in order to fulfil the request made to them by the Great Spirit. The intention is to awaken people not only to the existence of the World of Light but also to the relationship between that world and life upon the Earth and within our universe, as the actions of an individual affect the progress of the whole. Blue Mountain comes to teach the "Children of the Earth" the truth and reality of eternal life. He comes to impart the knowledge and understanding gained by the Brothers of White Light in a visual and audible form, and to deliver it with sincerity, simplicity and humour.

As he travels around the world he meets and greets people, inviting them to ask him questions and then helping them to learn and understand about his world and his people. The vision of him opens their eyes to new and exciting ideas, bringing about a different perspective of what life is all about. It creates for them a platform from which they can extend their knowledge and build a temple of peace, within which they can learn to communicate not only with life in the World of Light, but also with life upon the Earth and within the sky above us. All people in the World of Matter have companions like Blue Mountain, who are waiting to be acknowledged, so that they, too, may bring their friends out of their darkness (just as Blue Mountain brought Gayna out of hers) and into the light of pure Spirit Love.

For all people in the World of Matter it is important to know that, no matter what occurs around them, if their love is strong and deep enough it will carry them through eternal existence, surrounded by the illuminating light of the Great Spirit, the Creator of all life. The World of Light is the home of Blue Mountain and Gay. It is full of illumination, love, peace and tranquillity; there time is spent surrounded by beauty of the heart and of the soul. Many people on the Earth constantly place emphasis upon physical inadequacies. They fail to see the total adequacy of the Spirit, which permeates all of existence.

Every living soul on the Earth today has the ability to reach out and touch the 'lighted realms' and bask in the warmth and understanding of the companions who reside there. The hearts and minds of people are the gateway to their love!

Extract taken from the book: -
BLUE MOUNTAIN
Native American Spirit Teacher
AND GAY
"A True Story"
Re-written, in parts, for the benefit of the reader.

Blue Mountain's Story Continued

Blue Mountain, Ambassador for the World of Light.

Many times people will think to themselves, where am I going? Where is my life taking me? They may then begin to investigate their life; where they have been, where they now are and where they are going. So begins the unfolding of the mind in the searching for their future. Some people believe that there is far more to life than they have encountered, so they begin to think about life. What is life? Where does it come from?

There are those who turn to the standard religions for the answers to their questions, but there are many, growing in number, who are turning elsewhere for answers. They search amongst people. They search amongst books. They will talk to each other. They will talk, very often, to strangers. Then they will sit and think. At this time of contemplation the Companions beside them, from the World of Light, from my world, will come forwards, will begin to influence their actions and their direction.

My people are very aware of the needs of your people; of the requirements to provide all people with their individual answers. Many search for answers to their life of matter, and then there are others who will search for answers to the life of the Spirit.

I come to you to represent the World of Light, to represent the world where all people, all life, resides. You are Spirit here and now. My World of Light is Spirit. So you are all a part of my world. All life in the World of Matter is Spirit; the animals, the trees, the rivers, the birds in the sky. All are Spirit. All belong to the World of Light. By residing in this World of Matter you are experiencing a great variety of life, so allowing 'You', the Spirit, to broaden, to grow and develop.

Within my world, the important factor is the total expression of love. We gather together to emit energy to all that is around us. Within that energy there is the strength gained by the beings who engage in the transmittance of this energy.

Beside each one of you there is a Companion who is trying to help you. They are trying to guide your footsteps so that you tread the pathway of life with as little disturbance as possible. But all too often you fail to recognise this, because you say "I." "I do not want." "I do want." My friends get very confused sometimes, but remain beside you. They bring you courage to face the obstacles that are there for your benefit. They give you their love.

Very often during your life, you will carry out certain activities; you will work, you will play, you will have families. Some people may have hobbies. Many people, then, at the termination of their life, will believe that this is the end to all of the aforementioned; the end of their life, which is the total sum of all of their experiences, all their learning, all their pain and heartbreak. All their mistakes will be finalised at the time of termination. Very few people properly understand that it is not the end. Some people believe that they will continue, but in a shape and form that is very different from their condition now. Then there are the people who fully appreciate the continuation of life in a different dimension of energy. In this different dimension, all your experiences in this life will have consequences in the eternal life.

I come to you today, to emphasise that there is no death. 'Death' is only a word created by human beings for human beings. All of your words and actions in this life will have consequence in the eternal life, and you are responsible for your eternal life. There is no magic that will wipe away all of your comments and actions during your time here. No. When you eventually move to my World of Light you will see the results of your life. You will see all of the good and all of the bad. Then you will make judgement accordingly; judgement upon yourself. Your position in the eternal existence will be determined by your life here, now, just as your position prior to your arrival in this life was determined by your previous lifetimes in this World of Matter and in many other dimensions.

Many people fail to appreciate that, when they talk, it is important to think first. They allow their emotions to be in control of them. They will act and talk and then they will think. Many of your people will allow the words of other people to stir emotion within them. They will then turn and blame the other person. "Oh no, it is not my fault" they will say. "If that person had not said that, then I would not be as I am." All too often this occurs. Few people will accept responsibility for the harm that they themselves cause. All too often it belongs to the other party.

When you come to my world, then you will see. You will see the laughter that you have given to people. You will also see the hardship that you have given to other people. Then you will determine the place where you belong. Many people will mistakenly surround themselves in conditions that are unsuitable, because of the information delivered by your people in your world today; indeed, delivered over many, many years. I, today, would like to bring to you the truth and reality of the eternal life.

CHAPTER 2

Eternity

Throughout life, you walk along a pathway from A to B, from birth to death, and you walk around obstacles; boulders that you meet upon your journey. Very often, there are people who stand in your way. Through your deliberations; your thinking and your feelings, you will negotiate these obstacles, allowing you to continue your journey through life. Along this journey you will gain information and knowledge from books, from people and from your own experiences. As you tread this pathway your course of action, regarding certain situations, begins to change. No longer do you view life from the naivety of youth, but there comes around you, into your mind, into your thinking and your heart, a certain degree of wisdom. So the energy that you use, to negotiate your pathway of life, begins to be used with less aggression.

As you move through life and the years of age comes around your shoulders, so you pursue your goals with less haste, becoming slower and slower, more certain as you walk your pathway. Your footsteps become heavier upon this path. Then information will flow into your environment and you may find the fire within your heart begins to glow again. Passion begins to envelop your very being. It is then, within that glow, within that passion, that influences can begin to take hold; influences that have been outside your considerations through life.

Then you come to 'The End?' The termination is solid? It is there at the end of your journey, the 'death' that is known to your people, the end of the story, the end of 'The Book?' All of the knowledge and all of the experience; all of the people that you have encountered; all of the passion, the desires, the goals; all of this gone: no more. You have closed 'the book'. Where does 'the book' go? It goes into the ground, and upon it is laid a stone with the name and the years upon that stone.

So, the stone lies in the ground and, as the years go by, the winds come; the rain falls; the Sun shines; the flowers grow, then they fade away. The autumn comes, the leaves fall and then the snow lies upon the ground. The spring then arrives, the blossom falls, and so the cycle continues, for however many years. I cannot say for eternity, because there is the belief that there is no eternity, but 'the book' remains. The energy associated with this life is there, continuing to vibrate, continuing to exist, but for how many years?

I would, today, wish to place a seed within your mind. It is the concept of 'Eternity'. The ever-existing concept, the significance of the continuing vibration of the energy that is associated with the 'Book of Life' of the individual. Indeed, the physical vehicle, the body, remains in the soil, buried beneath the stone. The physical vehicle will, in time, disintegrate, but the Book of Life remains and will continue to have influence upon the energy of all other 'books'. Life will evolve. This world of yours, the World of Matter is growing, changing, just as the 'human beings' are evolving and changing, it is natural. But, certainly, within this evolvement there will be the birth of new life and then there will be the 'Book of Time', the 'Book of Experience', the 'book' associated with the experience of this life. This belongs to all who inhabit this planet, all 'Life'. Upon this planet, there are many hundreds of thousands of life-forms who inhabit this environment, all sitting together, side by side. When the time arrives, there will be the closing of the 'book', the 'death' that you know. But remember the seed that is **Eternity**.

When life first exists, it exists in its purest sense, then, it goes its own way. Life never totally returns to the source. Life always tries to manifest the source, always striving to reach this goal, to bring forwards the perfection that existed at the time of its creation. The existence of life from this point takes many different avenues.

There comes a time when certain experiences are provided for the Spirit to assist in bringing forwards this manifestation. A number of choices will require the existence and manifestation upon certain living environments. I choose not to use the word 'planet', because there are a number of existences that provide the image of a planet, but are not a planet as you would know. You would see a planet as being an obstacle within the universe that you are able to see, and yet there are many other living aspects that create the same image. These aspects are within different realms of vibrating energy.

So now the decision is being made for the life force that has been created; the decisions to allow this life force, Spirit, to gain its first manifestation within an environment that is alien to the perfection of its own existence. For your benefit, I will use, at this moment, the words 'planet removed'. To help you to understand, imagine an image of yourself without the physical vehicle; now you are seeing the equivalent of a 'Removed Planet' (a planet in energy form only). So Spirit begins its journey upon a 'removed planet', beginning to feel, beginning to experience the different vibrating energies that exist within all life, within all that manifests. As experiences begin to build, different and greater experiences come to the Spirit.

One experience is the physical environment. Within this environment there are different experiences, different planets where experiences can be gained; planets like your 'outer worlds', planets like the 'inner worlds', and like your own world. Life's journey is eternal. There is indeed no time, only existence. A multitude of experiences are available to Spirit.

If you now imagine blank pieces of music paper, you will see the lines upon which the music will be written. Now see 'You', Spirit, as a note being placed upon these lines. As your life begins, you begin to make music. Do you think that your tune will all be upon the one line? No, you will be moving down and up, down and up. Sometimes along, then down; along and then up. These lines are only a very small aspect of the music sheet. The music sheet is immeasurable. The lines are immeasurable, but, in order for you to create for yourself your own tune, that will depict 'You', you will be utilising all aspects of the music sheet.

There are laws that are associated with life and with the closing of the 'Book'. These laws are not dissimilar to your own laws of human existence. These laws belong to the universe. They exist whether you are here or not. They will continue to exist, even if this planet were to be removed tomorrow, because within eternity there are many, many other vibrations of energy. It is these vibrations that will continue to permeate eternity. These laws go beyond those of the human experience. They belong, as I have said, to all life.

The human being considers the human existence to be the primary form of life within all life. That is because you have evolved to a point of external creation, outside your own physical form. But this belief is untrue, because within eternity there are many, many forms of creation. They do not all occur outside the physical form. This may be contradictory to some, but it may fill the hearts of others, who open up to the greater experience of creativity.

There are many souls in my world who bring to you their love, who bring to you their vision and determination, their courage and strength, to assist you during your time in the World of Matter. Many of your people believe that there is no time after this life. But I know there are people now who are searching. They believe that there exists eternal life, but fail to recognise the reality of my world, the reality of my people. This is why I come to you as I do now, as I make effort to bring to you the reality of my people. They possess their likes and dislikes, like me. But I am like you. I am Spirit. You are Spirit. You and I, we come from the same source, from the Great Spirit. Your brothers and sisters, my brothers and sisters are all life. You are life. The animals are life. The trees, the grass and the soil, the rivers, the sky and the Sun; all are life.

Try to be gentle with the 'Children of the Earth'. Try to be patient, compassionate and tolerant of the lessons currently being learned by the 'children'. I refer to you all as 'children' in the schoolroom, learning your lessons, growing strong and developing. Each of you is tender. Each one of you requires gentleness and compassion. Each one of you requires the love of the Great Spirit and within everyone is the Great Spirit. So from each should come the love of the Great Spirit, but all too often you fail to recognise the creative source within each person, as always you try to control. You try to control yourselves and those around you; the animals, the rivers and the air, all being controlled by the human being. If each one of you were to recognise the love of the Great Spirit in each other, then I am sure, eventually, a peace and harmony would develop around your world, in countries where there is currently intolerance and anger to those who have a different colour, religion, or sex. As I also know men and women try to dominate each other, I would say there can always be balance if attempted by you and recognised by you. You are all equal. The animals are equal. All life existing on your world is equal. So the human beings would begin to appreciate the value of life, and there would then stop the premature termination of this valuable life.

You have the power to change your lives, to change your lifestyle. You have, within your grasp, the power of success, but do not limit your understanding of success, because I refer to the success of the Spirit. Many believe that this World of Matter is the only environment in which to live, so all that exists around them is all that matters. Their very nice car, that, in my opinion, should always be blue; their home; their bank account; their position in their employment; all of this, to some people, is of paramount importance. Many do not consider the needs of the family around them; the need for communication, love, understanding and kindness. So they reject 'time'. They do not give time because they are too busy building and building, so they keep their time for themselves. I know you may say to me, "I do this for them," but, if you turned and communicated with your family, how many of them would say to you, "I choose you?"

I fully appreciate the material environment that exists around you, because you are all manifesting in the World of Matter and around you are needed the goods of matter, but also remember that you are primarily Spirit. You need to consider the Spirit, because, when the time comes for you to move forwards into my world, then you take with you not the goods of matter, but the wealth of Spirit. I am very sorry, but you cannot take with you your nice blue car. A great shame, I know. You cannot take your colourful money, or the lamps that light up in your homes. You do take to my world the 'Jewels of the Heart'. You take the developed compassion and understanding. You take the developed love. The jewels of sacrifice adorn the person who gives their time to other people, so that all in my world can see that this person has given of themselves. By doing so, you will grow. You will mature as Spirit, and it is this that exists for all time.

It is 'You', the Spirit that continues throughout all eternity, throughout the universe, throughout the many planets. By releasing the 'Body of Matter', you can then penetrate the beautiful realms of my world. You can show all people the very essence of 'You'. No longer is there confusion. No longer do you stumble in the darkness, but you shine like little lights throughout the kingdoms of the Spirit.

CHAPTER 3

The Adventure Begins

There are two occasions when transition occurs: the time of coming to this World of Matter as a baby, and the time of coming to the World of Spirit. Death is a human expression of time that has been shrouded in mystery for centuries and centuries, but there is, in reality, no 'death' only life. It is a time of transition; of movement from one level of energy to another. As this process takes place, so the vision of the individual is opened and they are able to see a light that shines down towards them. Then it is the mind of the individual that will determine their surroundings when they reach their new home. This is why it is important for people to know that there is a world of life that exists beyond the veil that has been placed between the two worlds. This veil is a fine subtlety between vibrating levels of energy.

Your world is a very slow world of energy, because all that is around it is matter. Matter is dense and heavy. It allows all who come here to see and hear the same. When you transcend this level to the finer levels of the World of Spirit, you begin to see different views of life upon this planet, where there are thousands of life-forms.

When you come to my world all life-forms seem the same. There are no physical barriers between life as there are in this world. Here, in the World of Matter, your animals are seen differently to the human being, or the bird in the sky, because of matter. In my world there is light and all are seen as light, so respect is given to all forms of life, because all forms of life are equal. In this world they are not.

The larger you are the more superior you become, according to the thinking of the human being, but this is not so. There needs to be greater respect for life.

The World of Matter is a world governed by the movement of the planets: the Sun, the Moon within your skies, and the transition of the Earth within the sky environment. The human beings have developed a time period suitable for living conditions with this structure. When you move to the World of Light this structure no longer exists. You move to realms of energy, not to another planet governed by movement, and existence is according to vibration. There is a continual permeation of light that is within all, but there is no day and no night as you know here. Your day and night are governed by your Sun, your Moon and the movement of your planet. Within the World of Spirit there is no physical Sun. There is a light that is very beautiful. It encompasses our world all the time. There is no setting or rising of this light. It is permanent.

All that exists within my world exists through thought. We are not dependent on the production of certain elements, so water is not the water that you know and light is not the light that you know. The water is not wet. It is a substance that creates refreshment for all who encompass it. The light is warming for those who need warmth. It is cooling for all who need to be made cool. There is a warm hue that exists within this light, which provides great comfort for all people, unlike your world. When your Sun goes down many people, who need the substances created by this light, become depleted, because its physical presence is no longer there for them. Within my world there is no requirement for this, no physical necessity. All nourishment comes from around us and is created by thought. When a person begins to lose certain aspects of energy, they will encase themselves within the energy of the water substitute. This will provide replenishment for them.

When you move to the vibrating realms of light, you are then able to penetrate a number of energy lines, so being able to move between periods of time. You are able to access the past, the present and the future. The evolution of your world now has already been experienced. It has been created within the World of Light. The process is to be filtered through the realms of energy, through to the very slow vibrating realms of the World of Matter. As your evolution moves forwards so your structure of time will also move quicker, but your people are not fully understanding of the complications of increased energy, and this is now showing in the activities of the human beings around your world.

When you move from this World of Matter to the World of Spirit, you will take time to allow conditions around you to settle. You will be able to fulfil all of your dreams in the World of Spirit. Then there comes the time when it is necessary for you to see the results of your life. When you have done this, you will then move to the World of Light where you will join with the greatest powers that exist. There you will stay for as long as you choose. In the World of Light there is no time as you know now. Your life here, the experiences, the learning and growth will be added to the experiences, to the growth and learning from many other Spirit beings and together you will move forwards through existence.

In my world, there are also areas where we can go to be with the many animals. There are people who, whilst they are here in your World of Matter, desire to assist the animals. In my world, also, they desire to continue their assistance. There are special areas for these animals, and the children are encouraged to visit these spiritual beings, as they also contain Spirit. They enjoy their surroundings and they share their enjoyment with everyone.

My world does not change from your world. The people do not change. The only alteration is with your mind, for you become very aware that you no longer require your body. To continue in my world there is no need for a body, so your mind gains the knowledge of continued existence without the human vehicle in which you now travel. There is, however, a need for some form around you. This form takes the place of the vehicle. Very often you become surprised by your continuation. You are unable to see yourselves without a form, so you appear as form in order for your minds to become settled within your new surroundings. As time progresses you gain more knowledge within your mind. You learn that there is no need for continued form, so it is discarded. I know you now say, "What is left?" I say to you that 'You' are left. Discover yourself and you will know what continues.

In order to create a home in my world you need a fine mind, because it is your mind that is the tool for your creation. The greater your mind, the greater your creation, for you are the maker of your mind; you are the maker of yourself. Very often, in your world, you are able to hide your thoughts from those around you. When you no longer have form you are no longer able to hide. I have heard many say, "I am human." I say to you that you can try to improve your mind. Try to expand and learn. Very often, when you place your foot into my world great shock and disbelief occurs. Very often, too, it takes time to know of your continuation. I say to you, learn now and when the time arrives you will progress quickly in my world. Remember, 'You' continue; your vehicle does not. Learn about 'You'. Find the real 'You' and learn, also, to accept yourself, and then you will go far.

When people come to my world before their time, they require rest, because great disturbance occurs to the Spirit. So, in my world there are buildings designed to allow these people to gain balance and rest, and to gain knowledge of their surroundings. Very often there are people in my world who desire to assist in these circumstances. Your doctors and nurses, who come to my world, often desire to assist the troubled Spirit, so they attend at their side and provide healing by the transmittance of rays of colour. Many of these buildings are coloured in blue, and some of them in the pink of love. The effect of the rays of colour penetrates the Spirit, so the resting person feels the warmth and comfort of their surroundings whilst they sleep. When they have rested for their required period, which is determined by the comfort of the Spirit, they are able to leave the healing building and they have the opportunity to go to many of the schools of learning. At these places, there are Spirits who bring knowledge to those who do not know of their surroundings.

Also, people in my world are able to go to the schools and colleges of learning, for continued development. To these halls come the wise beings from the illumined realms of evolution. They bring with them knowledge of the environment that they inhabit. I would say to you that there are many different environments for the energies of the Spirit. There are many titles given to certain areas belonging to certain beings that exist. All is determined by the knowledge and understanding of the energy. I say energy, because when you return to my world you become energy in its finest form. So there are levels of energy. Each level is, in itself, a multitude of levels.

When you return to my world, you will be surrounded by the people whom you have loved and by people who love you and continue to do so. Then there is a time when you will see the positive and negative aspects of your life in this world. When you have seen, then you will move to the environment that will be suitable for your growth and development to date. There you may reside for some time to gain extra knowledge, extra development. You may then move further, and I say further and not higher, because you move forwards; you do not move upwards. Here, you may consider the term 'The Valley of the Spirit'. Here there is a greater knowledge and a greater understanding of the 'Perfection of the Spirit', but many, for varying reasons, fail to consider this environment. At the place known by your people as The Valley, where there is this deeper understanding, there may be desire to bring this understanding to souls who exist in the slower vibrating realms of the World of Light. I would say to you, from The Valley there are many teachers, many souls who bring knowledge, who come to help you.

Many who come to my world do not desire to alter themselves. I am quite sure that you have encountered, in your time, people who do not wish to alter themselves. In my world they do not change. So, information is brought to the World of Spirit from the illumined realms of evolution, to encourage the people to make effort to progress. This is their choice. They do not have to go to these buildings.

We live within varying degrees of vibrating energy. Your presence within that energy will be determined by your own vibration upon release from the World of Matter. A greater knowledge of the essence of Spirit, which is love, will alter your vibrations. The greater the input of this knowledge, the finer and finer your vibration will become, so allowing you to pass to a finer realm of energy. The finer this realm is, the greater the tests need to be for you to gain an even finer vibration. You will never stop learning, but your learning experience in the finer realms will be broader than here. In the finer realms of energy, you will encounter a broader experience with the Spirit of the Universe, and your learning will take place as part of a group known to many as the 'Soul Group'. For the group to progress there needs to be a common vibration. When learning takes place in the World of Light, the progress of the group will be achieved by the learning of the whole group.

The true manifestation is the Golden light that shines above all. Many believe the Golden light is the light of the angels that exist within the heavens. This is an understanding of your orthodox religions, but the Golden light belongs to the beings of advancement who come to watch your progress and to aid and assist the progress of your world. They bring with them great power and the golden glow of wisdom that helps them to help you. Great healing capacity is available to those people who centre their attention upon the Golden light. Those who recognise the significance of the Blue light will have available to them great capacity of humanity. For those who envelop themselves in the Purple light, they will then gain the understanding of the most illumined realms of my world. For all people, there is need for the balance and harmony of the green within their lives. For those with red, there needs to be the elements of the other colours. Red can be a difficult energy for some people. If used correctly, there is great power available to the individual.

There are a multitude of realms within the World of Light. The 'Golden Ones' reside very close to the White light. Within these realms there are many dimensions. As you see the stars in your sky, then you will see the dimensions that exist within the varying realms that exist. Now, can you count the stars in your sky? Many people see colours around them, but they do not look properly. They may glance and see no more, but colours are frequencies of energy that are very important to the Spirit. The Spirit, when released from the physical vehicle, will vibrate at a particular frequency of energy. That frequency will divulge certain colours to the onlooker. I would encourage you all to look; do not glance, but open your eyes. Allow your eyes to gain clarity, speak with truth and honesty and walk the path of the Great Spirit, the path of Love.

Then there may come a time when it is believed that a

greater experience will be of benefit to the 'Whole'. So there are then decisions to be made regarding the experience. You may choose to return to the World of Matter in order to gain greater knowledge and understanding that will be of benefit not only to yourself, but also to the 'Greater Being'. When the decision is made, then preparations need to be made regarding the circumstances and experiences required during the Earth life. During all this process you will be preparing yourself.

Then the time of transition will arrive and you will come to the World of Matter; the world of physical experience, where you will join with other beings, so that you can gain the qualities that belong to the Spirit and improve upon these qualities.

Prior to your arrival in this world, there will be arrangements made, by you, for certain events to occur during your time here. Beside you, at the time you make these arrangements, there will be a friend, who, whilst remaining in the World of Spirit, will agree to accompany you during your time here. They will guide you into the events that you have planned and stand beside you during every moment of your time here, to encourage you towards many of the events that will be necessary for your growth and learning, which you will very often try to pull away from.

When you make your transition from the World of Spirit to the World of Matter, trauma is created within the knowledge of the Spirit. So, when you begin to try to recall, very often there is difficulty. Only time of contemplation and meditation will eliminate this trauma, so opening the doors of the Spirit to the existence of the past life. Many people will never be able to penetrate, because of the bricks built within the mind by certain bodies in your world, bodies of religion, people who try to deny the previous existence. It will always be of benefit if the mind can remain open. When it begins to close then the initial trauma will remain.

The birthing process into this world is a very difficult process. The impregnation of the beliefs of the parents only adds to the difficulties for the Spirit. Today, the child is less affected by the beliefs of the parents.

Many years ago, the child would have all existing knowledge of the Spirit removed by indoctrination. Today, the knowledge is there to be found when they choose to look for it. My people, now, are trying to inform everyone of the existence of the World of Light. This will enable all people to gain a knowledge of the importance of this life in the World of Matter, upon the World of Light. When this knowledge is absorbed, then we hope that all individuals will allow the children to retain all knowledge that is part of them. If they are unable to retain this, then, with training, it can be brought to the conscious memory.

Some people will always deny the existence of previous lifetimes, because their understanding of the structure of life prevents their acceptance of this. Very often, this is because they do not wish to accept responsibility for their words and their deeds. If they had previous lifetimes, they believe there would then be lifetimes to come, and then their words and actions would have consequence upon the future. I say to you, this life now is not the beginning and it is not the end. All that has been will be. All that you do now and have done will have results in lifetimes to come.

When you come here, you are restricted in vision by the casing of the material vehicle, so you will not be fully aware of the true significance of the events that are taking place. You will, inevitably, put your human understanding into the decisions that you are making, and, if you are displeased with the view before you, you may turn away. So the Companion beside you will make great effort to turn you back towards the event, because they know the true importance of your journey through the event.

During your journey through this life, in your search for

truth and reality, in your quest for knowledge, you will be emanating a bright light from within you, from the Spirit. Many people in my world will be enticed by this emanation, and, when they see the efforts that you are making, they may try to be of assistance to you. So you will always come to this World of Matter with a Companion and, during your journey, you will 'take bread' with many from the World of Light.

When you make your choice to come to this world, you are choosing to come to a school, because the environment of this planet allows you to merge with different Spirit beings and Spirit in different forms. By allowing this mergence, you are encompassing different degrees, different levels of understanding and knowledge. So the school will teach many greater tolerance, patience and understanding. The school will teach you greater love.

The many who come to this world, come with specific experiences to encounter that will teach them certain aspects of love; certain degrees, also, because development will take place in degrees. No person can say, "This person has no love. This person has no patience." All Spirit possesses degrees of these qualities. When you come to this world, you are only a small part of your 'Total Self'. You are only a degree of the 'Total Spirit'. You come with qualities of personality and character to allow a greater refinement of these qualities. When you return to the World of Light you again join with the Total Spirit and your increased degrees of love will allow a finer refinement of 'You', the Spirit. There are, however, certain persons who come to carry out a specific job at the request of the Great Spirit, the greater power that enfolds all life. At a given time in the life cycle upon the World of Matter, this specific job will become known to these individuals, but, primarily, all life that now inhabits the World of Matter comes to learn in the school.

The Companion that is beside each one of you will be

monitoring your progress through your life. They will be monitoring your actions and your reactions, your words and your thoughts about the varying emotions resulting from events that will have occurred during your years. They will know the best direction for you to now walk.

So, I am saying to you go ahead and make your plans. Indeed, prepare for the coming years, but do not place all of your hopes upon the achievements that you are now planning for your life, because your pathway is pre-determined by you before you come to this World of Matter, to this 'Schoolroom'. You may be planning, as the human being in a physical environment, a certain pathway for yourself, but you do not know if this is the true and correct pathway for you. How many times have you planned a straight path and then found, in a short time, that your direction is turning corners that you have not seen? Very often these corners are hidden from you, because if you were to see the sudden direction change, then you may become concerned, because you will not know what is around the corner. So you might hold back, very often afraid, because people within your world today always like to see in front of them. This allows them to be in control of their lives. It is that which you are not in control of that is of the greatest learning for you, and I refer to the learning of the Spirit. It is always the Spirit that gains the experience, knowledge and wisdom, not the vehicle through which you manifest.

Many look upon the human vehicle as the aspect that takes all that life will throw at them, but it is not. This vehicle (body) that you are aware of is merely an instrument that will allow 'You', the Spirit, to move through the 'schoolroom of life'. It is here to allow 'You' to gain a physical experience, so learning all about the slow vibrations of energy that encompass your world. This allows 'You', the Spirit, to learn how to manifest the perfection of Spirit, which is love. When you were all created by the Great Spirit, you were all created to bring forwards this perfection, and in doing so you bring forwards the perfection of the 'Whole'. The Great Spirit that created all life is a greater force than all that exists. This greater force has power, power to bring into effect life, life being love.

CHAPTER 4

Awakening

So, you have arrived as Spirit. You have arrived upon a body of slow vibrating energy, this being the World of Matter. This slow energy exists because around the energy particles there is a material barrier, which creates restrictions. In these restrictions there is the experience that is available to all life; the experience of allowing the true perfection to be manifest despite the difficulties that are around you.

Many people today believe that this world is here for their pleasure, is here for their own use. They do not realise that it is here for all life to express the truth and reality of the Spirit. They do not realise that it is, in itself, life, living and breathing, growing as you all grow. It is not the rock (planet), but the Spirit that is within and around it that will grow. As you now see the human vehicle, so you see the physical vehicle of the planet, but within all of you, around all of you, there is the truth that the Spirit is primary. Indeed, around the World of Matter there is Spirit also, the Spirit being primary. The physical manifestation is secondary. All the planets within your universe are Spirit; their truth, their reality is that they are Spirit. Their Spirit is utilising the physical vehicle to manifest the love of the Spirit. All that you see, all that you know to be reality is indeed a non-reality. It is the Spirit that is the truth, and it is for you, knowing of the reality, to bring forwards this truth, to allow the perfection to be manifest through you. It is for you to begin your pathway upon a different level of understanding to that which you have previously understood.

So, now you need to revise the plans you may have made, because your future pathway has now turned the corner. You are now aware of the importance of the manifestation of Spirit, so you need to make allowances for this in your life. You need to begin the unfoldment of the Spirit, allowing the total control over your life to be released to the Spirit that is within and around you. Your life here, in this World of Matter, is only the blink of an eye. Your true life is the eternal existence of the Spirit. Work hard at providing the light of the Spirit, so that all people will see your knowledge, your experiences and your wisdom. When they see, then they will, in turn, make an effort to bring forwards the manifestation of their own Spirit.

There are many of your people, today, within your country, who are searching for the sunshine. They are searching for a glint of light that will take them forwards, out of the difficulties that exist within their life. Many of them do not know where to turn, or who to talk to. They are frustrated within their very being. They are confused within their mind, because they see around them great difficulties within their lives, within their environment and within the world itself. Many of them try to manoeuvre themselves around the many obstacles that are placed before them. In doing so, they tumble. They gain injury to their emotions, or to their physical vehicle. So they search, but they do not know where to go.

My people, from the World of Light, gather around now to bring direction and light into the lives of the people. We try to direct you along your individual pathway. If your pathway comes alongside a building where there is the gathering of my people, then you will be directed into this building, but, all too often, the words of help do not come. The guidance from the World of Matter is not there, because your people are focusing their attention upon the many toys of material life. Your people forget the requirements of the Spirit. It is the Spirit that is the primary element of life, not the vehicle, the body.

Within all life there is knowledge of the Spirit. There is only need to stimulate this knowledge for there to then be a very clear direction in front of all human beings, but all too often there is a veil placed in front of the eyes of people; the veil of toys. Your people do indeed move to my world upon the cessation of the human vehicle. My world is the 'world of life', the world of continued existence where there is further growth, further development of the Spirit. There is not the further development of the human existence. The human existence is only for this World of Matter, this world known to you as Earth.

This world that is your schoolroom will not help your physical vehicle. It will not help your material possessions. It helps only 'You', the Spirit. Many of your people fail to recognise this important factor, so they strive throughout their life for the acquisition of material benefit. They forget the great need for the food and water of the Spirit, which this World of Matter provides. Your people turn away, because there is the indoctrination of your bodies of power to the need, the requirement of material benefit. There is not a need; there is not a requirement; there is only personal desire, personal wants. I want this, I want that, my neighbour possesses what I want. How many of you listen to these words within your life? "I want a larger vehicle (car). I want more money, more possessions and a bigger house." You do not. The human existence wants; the Spirit needs, but your people forget the needs. They turn their attention only to the want, and so now there is great deprivation within your country, within your world, within all life.

Here, in this World of Matter, there is a void of knowledge and understanding of the reality of the truth of life. So we guide people like you to certain areas where communication can take place, only to find that there is a need within that environment for the 'Word' of Spirit. Yes, indeed, there is the demand for proof, but many of your people already know, within their hearts, of the existence of a continued life. They need knowledge and guidance from my people, but when they arrive for knowledge they have constantly placed in front of them proof, instead of knowledge. Always there is the desire for proof. Are you not, here, now, in your existence, proof of Spirit, proof of life? Surely then, you require the further knowledge and understanding of the purpose of life. Then why continue searching for proof? Every life form within this world is proof of life, of Spirit, of the Great Spirit. You all result from the Great Spirit, from the great power that exists within and around you.

My people are trying to talk to you. They are trying to bring to you the knowledge, the understanding of the need to respect all life. The need to cease the constant destruction of your world, so that your people and all life upon this planet can continue the lessons within the schoolroom; continue within an environment that is suitable to all life, and I state: All Life. Not only the human being, but also the animals, the trees, the birds within your skies, the flowers, the grass, the soil and water. All of this is life, but human beings are trying to manipulate the environments, manipulate the animals and the human beings in order to create a greater power for the individual. There is a concentration upon the singular and a forgetting of the importance of the 'Whole'.

Your world will survive if you all centre your attention upon the 'Whole', upon the needs and requirements of all that exists around you. So, when you begin to send your thoughts out to all life, then you begin the process of healing your own difficulties, because you begin to feed the power of the Great Spirit through you (Spirit) to Spirit (all life). Then there is the removal of the human frailty because you connect with the Greater Power.

I know many of you today are searching for information. You are searching for experiences that will help you to understand your lives. Many of you will go to a religious establishment, many will turn to science, and there are those who will turn to the unknown; unknown because your world, your people state that it is unknown. My people, from my world, would say to you that these people turn to the known, because it is within each and every person within your world. I am referring, of course, to the Spirit. I am referring to a life that is encompassing your life now, but, because you are residing in a world of physical matter, it is very difficult for you to attune yourselves to this life. So this is why my people come to you now. We are aware of the increasing interest in the World of Spirit. This interest comes because your world is in turmoil. Many lives are in turmoil, and no longer is there the steadfast belief in life, in the Great Spirit, known to your people as God.

In time gone by it was the belief in God that allowed people to sit within their lives with comfort. But, as time goes by, this is being eroded by events that are in your world today; by the ideals and ideas of people that have manifested over many years. Very slowly people have turned away from the establishment, because they desire to gain their own personal experience. Their lives are personal, as indeed your life is personal, is it not? To be understood only by you, because only you have trod the pathway of your life. No other person has been in your footsteps, and I refer not only to this life but also to the eternal life. Many of your people are in controversy over the eternal life. They believe in this life because they can see, feel, hear and touch this life, so they accept the experiences that they encompass within their life now. Then there are people who believe in the life after termination of the physical life. They understand this because they have had experiences relating to this life that I now refer to, but many people reject, out of hand, the lives of the past. Many say, "No this is not true," because they cannot place previous lifetimes within their understanding now. I say to you, this is not the beginning and it is not the end. Your life has existed before now and it will continue to exist into the future.

Spirit is the eternal life. This World of Matter does not instigate the existence of Spirit, so, therefore, it cannot be the beginning. Spirit instigation is within the eternal realms that are inter-penetrating your world now. Many experiences come to 'You', the Spirit, before you engage yourself in a period of time upon this World of Matter, which is merely a schoolroom. It is not the place of birth of the Spirit.

There may be many times when it will be suitable for you to visit the schoolroom of physical life, but you do not return as you are now. When you leave this World of Matter, you return to a 'Greater Being', the true Spirit, of which you are only a very small aspect. When you return, you will embed, within this 'Being', the experiences of your life now. These experiences will help the 'Greater Being' to grow, expand and progress. Some time later, there may be requirement for further experiences within this World of Matter, so, then, other aspects of the 'Greater Being' may manifest in this world. But, remember, in all aspects there is the residual knowledge of the 'Greater Being' and, therefore, knowledge of time gone by and time to come, as within the World of Spirit there is not the time structure that you know of now.

Your people are very limited in their knowledge of the 'Greater Being', of the greater knowledge. They limit themselves by their thinking. So I would say to anyone who utters the words "No, I cannot," why can you not? Many people will provide very colourful explanations of why they cannot. I would say that the "cannot" is within your mind, not within your being.

Your period of time within this World of Matter is designed for you to manifest 'You', the 'Greater Being', not you the human. You, the human, are limited. The 'Greater Being' is the greater manifestation of Spirit. Your world, your people, impregnates into you, from the beginning of your life in this world, the inability to push yourself. Many will say to the child, "No, you cannot. You are not old enough. You are not big enough. You do not have the knowledge. You do not have the capability." As you grow, so the people around you will very often say, "You can do this, but you cannot do that." How many times have you experienced this? The Spirit, which is the all-encompassing 'Greater Being', can do all. It has vast capability. Through the Spirit you have access to great 'Minds', to great 'Beings'. You have access to great knowledge and wisdom. Wisdom within yourself and within the universe, and knowledge within yourself and within your universe - but how many times do you attune yourself to this 'Greater Being'?

Many of your people in your world today rationalise, calculate, plan, but very rarely do they feel. I know, also, there are people who feel but do not think. They react without first considering the consequences. They react upon emotion that is within them. I would say to you, put the two together, and you will contact the 'Greater Being'. Many people separate the two. They either think, or they feel. It will take great courage, great control to place the two together. Only then will the truth of the heart come into play. This is how you contact the 'Greater Being'. If you utilise your thoughts and your feelings together, then you utilise your heart and you allow love to penetrate all that you do.

Many actions from the thoughts alone create disturbance for people, and likewise many actions from the emotions alone create disturbance for people. Only when the heart wraps around the two will you be manifesting the Spirit.

Allow yourselves to be moved by the great power that is around you. Try to limit your attempt to control your life. Remember that your physical existence will restrict your view of your life, your true life, the life of the Spirit.

There are 'Beings' around you who can see. They have the ability to help you if you allow them to, but, very often, your people will say, "I am going this way, because I have decided. I have planned. I know where this road takes me." What have you heard me say constantly? I have said 'I'. "I am going this way. I have decided. I have planned. I can see." I. I. I. 'I' is the greatest restriction around your people. My people, from the World of Light, can see the obstacles in front of you. Their job is either to guide you around or to send you straight towards these obstacles. You may see the obstacles and you may try to avoid them, but it is not good for you to avoid them. Very often they are there to help you learn. If they are there by the making of another human being, then the Companions will guide you around them, but, if they are there for your learning process, the Companions will guide you towards them. They will try to influence you, but very often it is difficult because you say "I." Allow yourself to be moved, to flow with the power that is engulfing you. Allow your life to be that of the river. It will have its turns; it will have its pebbles and boulders and waterfalls. When you flow, then all the difficulties around you will be lessened, because you will be allowing a greater influence to come around you.

I am aware that it is often difficult to allow life to lead you, and not you to lead life, but try. Do not say "I cannot," because you can, I know. I say to you, now, you can if you try! Many people will not try. My people from the World of Light always say success will come when you try. You may say, "I have tried but not succeeded." You have succeeded, because your success is in your trying. Your success is success of the Spirit. Do not always look for physical success. You are primarily Spirit. You are here as Spirit. You will return to the World of Spirit as Spirit. Your human coverage is only suitable for this world. It allows 'You' to manifest in a vibration of physical energy. Your successes and failures are all associated with the Spirit. Very often, they cannot be seen by you. "I tried to obtain this job. I tried to achieve this qualification. I failed." These are comments by many of your people, but how many of your people truly understand that these objectives were not necessarily meant for them? They will say, "I wanted that job. I wanted that qualification." Then the emotion will build inside them, and all around them will know of their dissatisfaction.

To manifest the perfection of Spirit is to try, and then to allow the outcome of the trying to flow around you and to bring around you happiness and love to all people. But many of your people place their own dissatisfaction upon the shoulders of all around them. This is why, today, you have much fighting amongst your people. There are nations fighting nations, human beings fighting animals, and human beings fighting nature and destroying everything around them, because of their own inner dissatisfaction with their life.

I say to you, on behalf of my people, the gaining of power, control and wealth is not the purpose of life in this World of Matter. The purpose is to allow the elements of the Spirit to manifest and to grow, to allow the 'jewels of the heart' to be transmitted to all life. These jewels are the jewels of Love: compassion, tolerance, patience, tenderness and kindness. But many people today are too busy building wealth for themselves; too busy to give their time to people, to give their time to life to assist in the building and the development of the combined life of this World of Matter.

In order to gain the greatest benefit, it is important to allow yourself, the Spirit, to merge and blend with the 'Total Spirit', Spirit here and now and Spirit in the World of

Light. By seeing, by acknowledging that you are Spirit you begin your pathway to the answers about life. You will then learn. You will gain experience that is brought to you by the Companions standing beside you.

So, people are searching for answers to their life. Those who search amongst the unknown will begin to see the greater aspects of their life, to see the greater importance of their life. When this is achieved, then they will see the greater aspects and importance of life around them.

My people come to encourage all of your people to search for the Spirit within and the greater Spirit. When you find Spirit, then you find love. You do not find conditional love, but you find truth, reality within love. You find that this love belongs to you and to all life. It belongs to the planet and to the universe. Love is the Great Spirit known to you as God.

CHAPTER 5

Your Spiritual Journey

Many people in difficulty within their lives centre their attention within themselves, upon their own problems. Then their problems grow and develop beyond their truth, beyond the reality that exists, so the pathway that they are treading becomes more and more difficult. Only when attention is focused outwards, to all Spirit, will the healing truly take place. When your attention moves from the human to the Spirit, then you will truly be in touch with yourself.

You are all Spirit. You all come from the Great Spirit, so you are all a part of each other. Imagine the trunk of a tree; and then there are the branches that are a part of the trunk, but all are a part of the 'Whole'. You are all branches of the Great Spirit. You are all responsible for each other, and you are responsible for yourself.

It is my desire to discuss openly with you about your thoughts. You may wonder why. You may have thoughts that you would not wish to be seen, or, if seen, would your thoughts create joy and excitement in those who view them?

The Great Spirit permeates all of existence as a pulsating, powerful force of love; therefore, we all have this force pulsating though our very being, through our very essence. Many human beings today encase this love in a field of energy, hiding this power, trying to control it, trying to harness this energy, which, very often feeds through the emotions. Often, the desire for logic and reason will be respected and emotion is considered out of control, unreasonable, without the ability to think, to rationalise or to be in control of oneself.

So, today, the human being is trying to copy the new technology, the machines of your world; trying to be efficient and controlled, practical and productive, whilst inside themselves there is a raging emotion, powering though their very essence. This emotion will seep through into the thoughts of the individual. From the thoughts will come the words and actions that will display to those around the desires and wishes of the individual. Behind the thoughts there is the motive. The motive will very often come from the emotion. It is this motive that is very, very important to you, the growing, developing Spirit; your understanding and reasoning of this emotion and your ability to place it accordingly. Many times people do not place their emotions accordingly, because they try to manipulate people around them. They try to control people, frequently resulting in deception.

So we have to ask ourselves, as growing Spirit beings, how truthful are we to our very essence? How much reality do we bring forwards into the environment that has been designed to provide for us a learning experience?

How often have you found that those who talk to you are actually thinking something different, and how often has this caused, for you, some discomfort? The human vehicle is very efficient at creating a mask to the reality that is connected to the power that pulsates through all life. This mask is a deception. This vehicle is not real. The only reality that exists is the power of Spirit, the power of love! But today many people are afraid of love, because this very, very strong power will always come with pain. The more you love, the more pain will come to you.

People in this world will often try to manipulate love for their own gain, so that they can control and build the power around themselves. This power is very, very beautiful. It is filling. It will warm every corner of your very being. Today many people are standing alone, in the cold, without family, without friends around them, because your people today are busy. Always going there, doing this, seeing that, not having time to stop and to talk. So, there are people who are being deprived of an energy that is meant to permeate throughout all life, and they will try to grasp this energy for themselves. They are lonely, hurt, very often afraid, and many of these people that I talk about are the children of your world. Today, the family is not there to feed this power to their children. Many of these children are left alone. Their families are always going here, rushing there, reading this and seeing that. No time to spend with one another and the children. So these children will grow into adolescence and, oh dear me.

I watch your people changing. I see the suffering that is feeding the people. If only your people would slow down and create time for each another. If only they would once again share their love. Allow this wonderful energy to permeate throughout the whole of life. It is seen in every aspect of the Earth's existence today. The respect for life is wanting. Your people today tear up the countryside, destroying the trees and the flowers, removing the habitat of the bird and the animals. "What for?" I ask. For the construction of environments that will accommodate speed and the vast buildings of commerce, where individuals can build for themselves the so-called wealth of the material, causing deprivation amongst many, many people. The acquisition of material wealth is considered, today, the God of your society. Today, your people forget the true Great Spirit, the 'Power of Love'.

Your thoughts are the access to this power, and in my world there is great, great love for your people. We do not require material gain. Our wealth is in the heart, and my people wish to share our wealth with you. This is why I come to talk to your people and to you today. Through your thoughts you can gain access to my people. We are there, standing, waiting for you; ready to be your friend; ready to be your light, shining ahead of you; if you would only allow our presence beside you.

Very often, we will stand back. We will watch you struggle, and feel your pain and anguish as you trip and fall over the many pebbles and boulders along the pathway of your journey through life. We will stand and cry for you, and hold out our hands to help you, but many in your world today will not open the doors to my world, through fear and apprehension. So we watch as you continue your struggle. But we can be a beacon of light, shining ahead of you through your life, so that when the boulders and pebbles come into view you are able, with our help, to sidestep and manoeuvre around these inevitabilities.

Every living being upon your planet has a Companion beside them. When loneliness, isolation and frustration comes to you, and you feel that there is no one there who understands, there are always my people, your Companions, who will place their arms around your shoulders so that their strength feeds through to you. We cannot remove your obstacles in life as they are there to help you learn. Not you the human being, no, but 'You' the Spirit.

The earthly life is short for all of you; it is merely the blink of an eye. The eternal life will move you through growth, through the development of your own soul and the development of the soul group that you belong to. The development, also, of all life, because you are all joined together as one and you are all growing as one. As all of existence is joined as one, when an individual creates pain for another, who is being hurt? All life is being hurt. Every small aspect of existence is being hurt because you are all one.

You are all from the Great Spirit, and at no time are you

separate from the Great Spirit. That pulsating energy permeates you all, feeding out and back, out and back, constantly creating movement and resulting in change as the energy moves and grows. So, when one being causes pain to another, pain feeds throughout the whole. This is why a greater respect is required for this planet. She, too, is a part of the 'Whole'. She, your 'Mother Earth', is a living, breathing Spirit being that is evolving, growing and changing. Constantly, the human being, through greed, power and control, harms the planet and therefore harms all life. This is another reason why I come to your people. Many of my colleagues also try to talk to your people. We are trying to clean the windows of the mind, so that you can see the consequences of your many actions and words.

You are not living alone; you are living with all of us, including me. I can see you but I am not in the material environment. I can touch you with my energy. I can feel your energy field and I can touch the vibrations of energy. I can also hear you, and I wish for you to open the window of your mind and to allow communication to flow between our two worlds. We care about you. We love you. We care about all of life. We love life. We are all from the Great Spirit that loves and protects all: no prejudice, no jealousy or greed, only love.

Your thoughts manifest energy. By constant negativity being developed within you, you are transmitting negativity to the people around you, and they, in turn, will transmit this energy to others. So there begins a chain of events from you around all life. It is, I agree, very difficult to centre your attention upon the positive aspects of your life when you are engulfed in pain and suffering, but you are capable. You have the facility to find within your life one small positive element. I will give you one element: you are alive and experiencing the power of Spirit around you. You are in contact with others.

By the centring of your sight upon another life form, you are witnessing the great power of Spirit, so you are witnessing the Great Spirit, the power known to you as God. God is within your life, so great beauty is manifesting now in front of you. You see the trees growing, you see the animals around you and you see one another. You are seeing the greatest power that exists within your universe. You are touching this power. The problem will very often arise when you try to hold onto the power, as doing this will cause your fingers to begin to burn. The power of the Great Spirit is to be fed from Spirit, through Spirit, to Spirit. It is fluid, ever moving, ever touching all that is around. When you try to control, then you place limitations around you. Then 'You', the Spirit, cannot breathe correctly.

Your people, within your world today, constantly desire control. They desire power to benefit the 'One' and not the 'Whole'. There is no respect for life or the Great Spirit. There is now, manifesting within your world, greed, jealousy and hatred within the hearts of the human being. There is a requirement now to disperse these elements of human existence, because your world is changing. It is trying to evolve. As your people have evolved they have forgotten the planet. They reap the planet of all of its nourishment and forget love. Your people forget love.

The Great Spirit is Love! My people, from the World of Light, always come to you with love. Without this element there would not be life, so we come to you now, as I come to you, to bring to you love. Within your lives there are holes. These holes need to be filled with love. When they are, then you will be filled and you will be able to transmit this very element to other beings. I would like you to help me and my people by transmitting love to your people.

Around your world, there are people who are trying to destroy the work of good being accomplished by others, for their own personal benefit. Many allow the negative emotions to come forwards because of jealousy; because they do not hold the power that others possess, so they feel deprived. They feel the power belongs to them, with very little thought being given to their own deserving.

For the human being, overpowering negative emotions are very difficult, because you are encased within the physical vehicle, the vehicle that is so necessary to your manifestation within this World of Matter. You are all primarily Spirit. You have chosen to come to this world in order to gain certain experiences. In order for you to do this, it is necessary for you to take on board the human form. So the channel to this higher being is restricted because of the very heavy particles of energy, of the 'vehicle of matter', the body.

Your time here, in this world, is designed for you to find and put into practice the true reality of yourself. Many people choose not to do so. They encase themselves within the pleasures of the World of Matter. When they do this, they are allowing the very base emotions to manifest, so allowing the energy around them to become slower and slower. These persons are encouraging the very heaviest of energy.

It is the Spirit, the very essence of the World of Light that produces the finer vibrations of energy. For many people, the achievement of these finer vibrations is beyond their reach only because of their perception, their own attitude to life and to themselves. So they embed themselves in the negative emotions that exist within all people.

When 'You', the Spirit, begin your journey along the pathway to the Great Spirit, you are placing with yourself great responsibility to uphold the Laws of the Universe, the Law of the Great Spirit, which is the Law of Love. You will be falling short if you allow the emotions of greed, jealousy and hatred to come forwards. It is your responsibility to bring forwards, to the front, the emotions of compassion, kindness, tolerance and love.

Many people place their own life within the lives of other people, so they begin to make judgements of people they do not know. They fail to manifest tolerance and understanding. These are the 'jewels of the heart'. Many people consider what is not really there and make judgements. They make decisions based on what they do not see, because they believe they have the knowledge. They believe the power belongs with them. Only one power truly exists; this is the power of love. My people, from the World of Light, are now trying to encourage the peoples of your world to take grasp of the true power and to direct it to all life without prejudice or judgement, without saying, "This 'Being' deserves and this 'Being' does not."

I come to encourage you to take the power with you into your home and your place of work and to allow the love to flow through you. Allow the Great Spirit to become a part of your life. Your life is the life of Spirit, because each one of you is Spirit. Admittedly, you should allow the human emotions to be acknowledged, but then place them in their true perspective: place them secondary to the Spirit. Do not manifest the negative emotions, the negative energy, but allow them to be. You will not be able to wipe them away, because they belong to this World of Matter in its current state.

How many of you look at yourselves? I do not refer to the looking glass; I refer to the true 'You'. How many of you know yourselves? How many of you believe yourselves to be someone different? Many of your people today look superficially at their surroundings, at themselves, at people around them. Very few actually take time to delve into themselves. Many people are too busy carrying out their daily activities, going to their place of work, dealing with their home conditions, considering all around them but themselves. I do not refer to the material pleasures of themselves, but to time being taken to really discover the true personality, the true being that is within and a part of the Self. Within the cover that you see, the vehicle (the body), there is Spirit. Many people believe implicitly that, when searching for Spirit, they search outside of themselves. They do not appreciate the importance of Spirit within. You are a part of the world that you seek. I wish to encourage you to begin your search from within. Take time to discover Spirit. Each day, make time for yourself. Find a period when you can sit and communicate with Spirit, communicate with yourself.

Many of your religions, in your world today, talk about the 'talking to God'. They say, "God is around you; God can be spoken to; talk to God – who very often belongs in the sky – and you will get your questions answered." The truth, the reality is that God, the Great Spirit, is within you. Talk to yourself. Discover the great abilities that belong with you. Discover all of the knowledge that is within you, and you will be starting your pathway to the Great Spirit. The Great Spirit is around you, indeed, in the skies. All that you see is the Great Spirit but, very often, the one area you do not see is yourself. Many people say to me, "How do I talk to Spirit? How do I know that Spirit is talking to me? How do I recognise the difference?" I say to you, there is no difference. You are Spirit. Many people seek guidance and advice from the World of Light and I commend the desire for this but, very often the greatest assistance can be gained from you.

There are two areas of knowledge about you, about your pathway. One area is the Companions that stand beside you. They have knowledge of the life that has been designed for you. They will make effort to guide and assist you along this difficult pathway. The second area is you, because prior to inhabiting this World of Matter you took time to plan your life. Then people come to this world and they forget the great amount of effort put, by themselves, into the planning of their life. Many people expect answers to come from this area and that area, from this person and that person. When answers do not come they get disillusioned. They become troubled and angry because people will not tell them what to do, how to avoid this problem, how to solve that problem.

I would say to you, look at yourself. If there is a problem, it began with you and it will finish with you. Many people avoid making decisions, because of the pain it may involve, because of the difficulties that may be encountered as a result of certain decisions. But only you can achieve the balance and harmony, the peace within you. Many people will try to hide themselves away. Allow yourself to come forwards. Allow the truth, the reality, to talk through you. Allow your own Spirit to be your teacher. When you begin to accomplish this task, then a greater channel will be available to the Companions beside you, because the greater the knowledge that you can draw from yourself, the greater the field of energy will expand and grow. At this time, the Companions will be able to step forwards and merge their energy with your own energy, and it is at this time that communication with the Great Spirit can be achieved. Allow yourself to develop as the channel, then, allow the Companions to work with you, to work in the fashion that they know to be correct not the fashion that you choose.

Many of your people place great emphasis upon control; control over their lives, over people, over the environment and the animals. So they will say, "I do not like that." "I want this and I want that." When these wants do not come to them, their anger, their resentment and their disharmony begins to build inside them. If they were to say, "I am here and I will be the channel for the Power," the correct pathway would stand in front of them. The direction will come to them, very often from an area they have not seen, because they have not been looking. They restrict their vision to this and this, and not that.

Many people, today, have the facility to be a great power for the World of Matter, to aid and assist in its change of vibration. But many of the people are lost, because their area of power is not in accordance with their own desire, their own wants, their own need for control, so they turn away. This is not good because your world needs you.

I would say to you, begin by discovering 'You', the Spirit. Through this discovery you will become a greater channel. Then allow the Companions to move into this channel and to feed information to the people of your world. Through this feeding process there will build a knowledge of the truth and reality, and from truth will come light. The greater the light, the greater the influence from the World of Light; from the 'Masters', from the 'Minds of your Universe'. Your people need help and guidance. Allow yourselves to become a part of the progress by beginning with 'You'.

Many times you will need to go within for advice, to your own Spirit. Very often, 'You', the Spirit, will be able to assist you in your direction when you need advice and guidance; then you will be able to help yourself. Great benefit will be gained if you turn within yourself to the very essence of life. Turn to the Spirit, to the light that is within each one of you. The true light of Spirit is Love! Many people forget the importance of love. They are very often too busy dealing with their life-styles: handling their money, mending the vehicles, shopping, choosing their new clothes. Many forget that all the elements of love are of greatest importance; the elements of: compassion, kindness, patience, tolerance, understanding, and love itself. When you begin to connect with this light, your everyday occurrences will become more balanced and harmonious. So, the emphasis of living, gradually moves away from the elements of matter to the elements of Spirit. By achieving this movement there will be a harmony within and around you, so your life begins to change. Your life begins to move with smoothness. There is a flow to all activities that are a part of you.

You are placed here to learn lessons. These lessons, very often, will not be easy, but they will become easier to contend with if there is a balance and harmony within yourself, a connection between 'You', the Spirit and you the human being. The vehicle belongs to this World of Matter. It allows 'You' to manifest within the boundaries of this environment, so that you, as individuals, can gain experience. When you have gained this experience you will return to the World of Light. There, your individuality will be blended with a 'Greater Being' and will become a part of many 'Greater Beings', so a blending of minds takes place. All the experiences blend together, and this then allows the 'Greater Mind' to progress, through the realms of colour, towards the great light. These realms of colour also provide experiences that are associated with the colour.

Many of your people now are learning the significance of the colour of energy. When you return to the World of Light then a greater significance begins to take effect. It is through your understanding now, within this restricted environment, that you gain your greatest development, because your restrictions allow 'You', the Spirit, to push and push, so releasing the boundaries around you. Only when you are restricted do you fully appreciate the freedom that is open to you. So you begin to push for this freedom, for the removal of boundaries around you. These boundaries may be of the Spirit. They may also be of the vehicle, the human existence. Many people feel pressured by circumstances around them; by people, by their environment, by their work and by their individual lifestyles. Many people also feel pressured by themselves; by their own expectations, goals and desires, or by their own control of life and all that is around them.

When you begin to relinquish control, the power of the Spirit that is within and around you can engulf you. This power has greater influence, greater observation and greater knowledge. Many human beings believe themselves to be this power. They forget that they are only individuals. They are, as such, elements belonging to a greater power, a greater 'Whole', with greater significance around them. Many of your people misuse this control. So, around you, you now see the destruction of life, the destruction of the environment: the trees, the animals, the water in your rivers and oceans, and the atmosphere. Remember, it is the environment and all that is a part of it that allows you to function, allows you the privilege of residing upon this very beautiful 'Life Force'. I, of course, refer to the planet. She is a living, breathing 'Being', providing for all upon her, the elements of existence to allow the Spirit to grow. She provides the restrictions for you as individuals to push away, so creating a greater Spirit, allowing you to return to the 'Whole' a greater being. It is for you, as individuals, to attempt to become this greater being.

So, begin to search for the power of the Spirit within yourself, within your own life. Then you will be able to find this power within all life. When you have found it within yourself, you will then know that it exists within all life. When you have touched it, when you have felt the love that is a part of it, then you will know the true meaning of love and you will find it within all life. You will then respect life; you will respect all that is, all that you can see and all that you cannot. Do not be afraid, for beside you there are Companions, as I stand beside Tywane. These Companions will guide you. They will give to you the strength and the courage that you will need, because, to seek this power you will need to go into the greatest darkness.

CHAPTER 6

Life's Challenges

For some of you, the experience of releasing your desires for control will be emotional, because you have embedded yourselves in the emotions of solidity within your life; solidity of your circumstances, solidity of what happens to you. Around all of this will be the emotion that is built upon all that is. When you release control, then you release emotions. The more control you take away, the greater the emotions that are released, and I will specify one particular emotion, fear. Fear is embedded into all life: fear of the predator by the animal, the bird and the insect; fear, by the human being, of the consequences of being out of control, and fear of the emotions released when being out of control.

I am aware that releasing these emotions can be an upsetting experience. Very often, people will impart the emotion itself upon the shoulders of other human beings, but it is only the fullness of the emotion that should be imparted, not the fundamental aspect of that emotion. When you allow your inner pain to explode in anger at those you love, then you will be pushing them away. They will begin to build barriers and you will fail to achieve total support from these people. If you control this anger and quietly search for answers, then they, your friends and family, will turn to you, will hold out their hands and try to assist. They, because they love you, will wish to support you and will know your pain without the public display. The emotion is for you to learn about, for you to experience.

When you see a child in danger there will be emotion

within you, but it will be of no benefit displaying that emotion to others. It is of benefit for you to act upon that emotion by removing the child from the danger or the danger from the child with dignity, speed, determination and with courage, with respect for all that is around you. All of this is the learning process belonging to 'You', Spirit, within the confines of the human vehicle, for you to learn to manifest this perfection. As human beings you will very often make error in your judgement. If you then recognise this error then you will learn. If you deny the error and you place blame onto the shoulders of other people, then you do not learn.

Very often, when you are out of control the experience is very enlightening, because you begin to see a part of yourself that you have tried to hide for a long time; a part that you try to deny, try to move away from, because often you cannot place the emotion. It is uncomfortable for you, so you disguise, you dismiss, you wall up; but when you let go of this control, then it comes forwards and you then see you. You see you in all of your splendour. You see you the human being. You are here to manifest the perfection of Spirit through the human vehicle and all that the vehicle encompasses. The vehicle is the restricting element that will push you even harder to try to find the perfection.

Many people are satisfied with what they have. They do not realise that there is always a greater part of themselves. If you look, if you penetrate, you will then find a more beautiful self. When you see this beautiful self you will be able to manifest the greater perfection, but in seeing the greater beauty you will also find the stronger emotions of the human being.

Many emotions come to you because you are encased in matter. The matter fails to allow you to raise your vibrations sufficiently to find the true Spirit. The true Spirit would say to you, "Bring balance into the emotions." The World of

Matter prevents you from knowing this at the time of the emotion. So the physical brings forwards, for you, the many negative emotions belonging to the human being.

Many of you, when you feel emotional, when you feel greatly distressed, cannot bring yourselves to communicate with my people in my world. This is because, as your emotions become strong within you, you reduce your energy that is around you. You withdraw the field of communication, so my people have great difficulty in talking with you. At this time, you should try to communicate with your own Spirit, which has power like the 'Whole' has power. You will be making the first connection to the 'Whole' by communicating with yourself.

Many people, in their distress, talk and talk and talk, to this person, to this person and to this person. In doing so, they get answer A from here, answer B from here and answer M from here. I do not know about you, but I would be very confused with all these people giving different answers to me. I would be saying, "Which do I chose?" I would be most frightened by this confusion, but remember, all these people are trying to help you. They are trying to give to you their power and energy to help you. So they are feeding to you the power of the Great Spirit, the power of love, which is compassion and caring, because they love you, but many of your people do not recognise this power. They turn away from it because they are too emotional. At this time, if you were to go quietly and connect with yourself, with 'You' the Spirit and not you the human being, then you would be slowly opening your energy to the greater influence of the Companions around you and from them to the Great Spirit.

Many in your world today do not believe in my people; they do not believe in my world. When difficulties begin they allow their emotions to dictate their actions. So you see in your society many disturbances, great violence, anger and aggression. Many fail to allow themselves to rise above the emotion. Within the human being there is always emotion, but the desired pathway is to place emotion together with either thought or feelings. When I refer to feelings I talk of sensitivity: the sensitivity of the Spirit.

You reside in a World of Matter where these emotions are ingrained. As you grow, as you develop the Spirit and allow the Spirit to stand in front of the human being, these emotions will become controlled and understood. You will begin, then, to find alternative methods of communication. You will begin to try to find the balance between the thoughts and the emotions. When this balance is achieved, then you will begin to talk with the heart. You will begin to work with the Spirit, allowing the Great Spirit to shine from within you, outwards to all people who walk towards you. They will learn from you. They will see your countenance. They will see the balance within you and they will wish to receive the same, because as you work with the Spirit, so you gain a strength of energy that will be around you. This strength will assist you in walking the pathway to the 'Light', to the Great Spirit.

As you walk, you begin to work with compassion, kindness, tolerance, patience and understanding, and I do know how very, very difficult it is for you to work with patience in this world. We, in the World of Light, are not insensitive to your challenges in life, and when we stand and watch you successfully working in your life we admire you. We congratulate your efforts, and I would say to you the greatest achievement for you is when you try. When you do not try, then we say you need to work harder. It is in the trying that you will gain your greatest achievements, and the trying may only be a small step in your eyes, but this is greater than the apparent strides and jumps of easy accomplishments.

There is a need to respect the life of the planet in order

to gain respect for yourself, because you are a part of the planet. If you do not respect the planet then you cannot respect yourself. Within all people there are human frailties. These frailties arrive as a result of the restrictions of the physical environment, the energy of matter. You are not able to bring forwards the greater element of the Spirit that you, the individual, are. So you are able to manifest only a very small part of the true 'You'.

As a result of the human frailties, there will be within all people the element of ego, known to you all as the 'importance of the self'. Not the respect of the self, but the importance of self. Many recognise and accept that this is a part of them, and they make effort to place this element in balance with all aspects of the person. Other people find great pleasure in the building of the ego, because it provides for them the false understanding of their superiority to other beings. There will always be people who have this false understanding. Many times we try to provide lessons that will break down this false understanding, but, unfortunately, your world has many establishments that will encourage falsehood in many aspects of life. Only with the continued learning of the Spirit will there be the breaking down of the false understanding. I refer, of course, to continued learning in the eternal existence, not always within this world.

Beside you there are people in your life. You see their vehicle; you do not see their Spirit, but the Spirit is the primary element of life. Your vehicle is designed for you to express your consciousness within this World of Matter. It is a machine. It functions upon the direct influence of the thoughts within the mind. The mind is the Spirit. When you experience certain events you may become emotional. Your emotions are not solely determined by your life here. Your Spirit will encompass emotions and experiences over your 'total life'. Many people will turn to you and they will say to you, causing pain and confusion, "You do not know how I feel; you have never experienced what I am going through." Your pain and confusion is as a result of your experience of emotions, that people now say you should not possess. As you now wonder where the emotion comes from, I would say to you these emotions are as a result of 'total life' experience. So people cannot judge you, as they have not moved in your footsteps of life. They have not experienced your 'total life' and they never will be able to do this.

The people who walk with you through your life do not completely understand the programming of your life, but the people in my world do understand. They have prepared your life before you enter this World of Matter. Together with you, they have organised a direction along which your life will take you, but the people in your World of Matter have not necessarily been a part of this organisation. So, in their effort to assist you they may try to guide you along the wrong pathway, along their own pathway. My people know your pathway, your direction. The Companion standing beside you knows what is best for you the individual, because you are an individual, with individual purpose and direction. Also, you are Spirit. You have a connection with the Great Spirit.

I know many of you often feel your lives are very difficult. You often find yourselves moving in one direction and then, without seeing, you suddenly turn towards another direction. So, for a period of time you feel lost. You feel confused and, very often, this will result in a changing of emotion. I know that at this time you despair. You fall out with your friends, with your relatives, with the people closest around you. They will try to help but this may only cause for you more confusion and greater disturbance. I say to you, it is at this time when you should turn to my people. Turn to the Spirit, to the Companions and friends that are around you from my world.

When times of trouble arrive and you become emotional, you are often unable to be quiet and still. You are unable to obtain for yourself the necessary harmony and balance, which is required in order for you to receive the correct information from your Spirit. I would say to you, at this time it will be your Companion who will be able to assist you. I say this because your Companion, having been with you for a long period of time, is able to match your emotion, so bringing to you the necessary advice and guidance through your mind. When times of trouble come to you, as they often do, I would like you to talk to your Companion.

Emotion is part of the Spirit, but, very often the encasement of matter reduces your ability to gain information from the higher aspects of your Spirit. Each one of you is only a part of the whole Spirit. Each one of you is part of a higher aspect of Spirit. By coming to your World of Matter you leave behind a large part of yourself; you leave behind 'You'. Many of your people today do not like themselves, because they only see the large negative aspect of themselves. Many, as a result, take their discontent out on their fellow human beings. I would say to you, start to discover 'You' the Spirit and not you the human being.

Within each one of you there is an aspect of the Great Spirit, and when joined with the 'Collective Spirit' you become whole. Many of you are only associated with the Spirit of yourself, with the Spirit of the Companions around you and with the people in your world, but there is also the greater aspect of Spirit. Many of your people only connect with a small part of the 'Whole' so, very often, feeling confused, empty and afraid. I would advise you to make effort to unite yourself with the 'Whole'. Unite with the mountains, the rivers, the birds that fly in your sky, the trees that your people so heavily destroy, the blade of grass beneath your foot, the clouds in the sky, and the children of your world who are also Spirit. When you do so then the light will shine upon you. When this light shines upon you then you begin to bask in the power, the 'Power of the Spirit'.

For many of you I see within your heart the questioning; the enquiries; the searching for knowledge, truth and reality. I would say to you, all of this is within you. All is within your heart. Many of your people search around themselves. Many will go a long way to try and find this truth, to try and find the very essence of life. They will search through books and they will talk to many people. Then, after a time, they become very disillusioned, because they do not feel that they find truth in many of the answers given to them by other people. I know many will say to me, "Why do I not sense this truth? Why can I not feel this reality?" I would say to all who talk to me, "Because it is not a part of you." You are searching along another person's pathway. You are gaining another person's truth and reality.

Each one of you comes from a different direction, along a different pathway, and I refer to the pathway of life. Not only this life now but also the 'Eternal Life', the 'Eternal Pathway' that is for all people. You are all walking along different pathways, but you are, also, all walking towards the one source, to the Great Spirit. This Great Spirit is within and around you. It is a part of you, but your individual truth, your individual reality is a part of your own experience, a part of your own lessons. So, you will be approaching the same truth from a different direction and, therefore, from a different perspective. For some people this is fluid; for others it is more solid. For those with fluidity, other people's answers may be satisfactory, but for some, their own experiences, their own lessons are more solid and real to them. So for you, my friend, I would say your truth, your reality will come from the heart, from within you.

There is no limit to the continued life of consciousness. You continue to gain experiences in my world as you do in your world. You choose: to return to this World of Matter; to reside in the vehicle that you have chosen; your family and friends; and the environment that you now live within, before you arrive upon this planet. Also, you choose the experiences that will enable you to gain growth and development of the Spirit. During your time here you will be required to face these experiences. Many of you, I know, would choose to turn away from these experiences, but there are those in my world who come with you, who stand beside you and assist in your development. They assist you to engage with the experiences that you have chosen. They know that you will develop and gain growth from these times.

Very often, these times will create pain and suffering. In your pain, in your sorrow, you will experience emotions. Your reactions to these emotions will result in growth. I know many of you will say to me, "Why do I need to experience pain? Why can I not gain the growth without pain?" I desire to say to you that without the pain, without the suffering, you would not know the joy of the light. From the darkness comes the light. Without experiencing the darkness you would not recognise the light. From your pain and suffering you are also able to assist those around you who suffer also.

Very often there is ignorance - a lack of understanding within a person - and a lack of feeling, a feeling of the pain of other people. Empathy is required to develop and expand. Sometimes, people are cruel and they know what they are doing. This occurs through greed, through control and the desire for power. These people do not fully appreciate the far-reaching consequences of their words and actions. Words are like arrows into the heart. Once fired they may be removed, but the hole, the wound is always there. Always be very careful of the words you say. So, there is cruelty, but there is the power within the hands of all people to wipe out this cruelty. This power is available to every single person.

Pain comes to you from different sources: from the experiences of your own learning and also from the hard words and actions of other people. So you gain pain from yourself and you gain pain from others. Pain from others can be avoided in two ways. One way is for you to stand back from the experiences of the other person; to detach yourself and not become involved in the troubles of other people, even though they may want to involve you. Secondly, the people can control themselves. They can listen to their words of harshness and look at their actions that cause you pain. So we have two ways for you to become healed from outside pain.

Now we turn to the pain caused by yourself. This is less easy because, very often the lessons of life, the exams that come to you, are there for your benefit and they may indeed cause pain to you. If you were to sit in a garden of roses for years and years, would you fully appreciate the beauty and fragrance of the view? If you were to be placed within the environment of the desert for a year and then returned to the garden of roses, would you then fully appreciate the beauty and fragrance of that garden? So there are obstacles in front of you that cause you great pain, great suffering. These are for you to gain your learning.

I would say to you, at this time you are not alone. My people stand beside each one of you. They give to you their strength and their courage, for you to walk forwards along your dark pathway. They, very often, will cloak you in their own energy, to help protect you from the bitter cold winds and the rain that will fall upon you from time to time. How will the rose grow and blossom if it only experiences the sunshine? The rose needs nourishment, it needs the rain for food and water and it needs the wind to test its strength. Then the Sun will shine, and this will help the bloom open, to give fragrance to all who gaze upon it.

CHAPTER 7

The Pathway to Wisdom

When you come here, you agree to join with 'Beings' who are not upon your frequency of energy. This world is an environment that is suitable to many aspects of life, from many different areas of Spirit.

During your eternal life, there will be times when you have been of benefit to life and times when you have not. For your further progression, it will be important for you to balance the effects of your benefit. There may be times when you are about to proceed within my world but, in order for you to do so, you will need to return to this life to provide balance, because your benefit to life may be to life-forms that do not exist around you in my world. So, you are able to come to a gathering place, an environment where all energy can join together upon the same frequency.

The difficulties in your life here are pre-programmed by you. Some of the boulders are for you to learn. Some are for you to create balance. Whilst you are here you will not know, because it is designed for you to create the balance within the same conditions as the previous imbalance. So, some people may come to serve, some may come and encompass the problems of personal relationships, and some will come with the difficulties of the human vehicle. Everything is agreed by you before your arrival.

No person can determine the problems and difficulties of another person. "Why?" I hear you say. I would say that it is because you have not lived their life. You do not know the true level of their progression of Spirit. To you, your neighbour is in great difficulty with their life, but to your neighbour this may not be the difficulty that you can see. You may be to one person the pupil and to another person you may be the teacher, but in this world of single vibration you do not know, because you cannot see the different vibrating aspects of Spirit.

Try now to accept responsibility for yourself. Try not to remove your emotion from yourself onto other people. Do not place responsibility with other people. You will find, when you come to my world, that your actions have had consequence. Your lifetimes to come will be planned according to how you have conducted yourself in lifetimes gone by. You will find the cycle of karma will be around you. Try to bring forwards compassion and understanding when other people do not act as you would wish them to. Try to find in your heart forgiveness, as this will remove the cycle of karma between you and another 'being', then you will be able to move forwards in this life and your eternal life.

I say to you, progress does not stand still. Do not become satisfied with the level of attainment already acquired. There is great potential within your people. Search for the wisdom needed to take you further. Knowledge of a certain amount is not enough, you need to expand your minds.

Around your country there are those who do not possess your knowledge or your understanding, because not everyone has the same experiences as others. Instead, they gain their knowledge of the experience from the words of those around them. I know, not all of you experience the same as others. In order for you to progress you need to build on your own experiences. Do not be content to stay where you are; you must learn more, progress further. I know you will do this. You are searching, wishing to gain the experiences placed upon your pathway, but do not discard the knowledge or experiences of those around you.

Your learning does not only come from your physical experiences. Search for your information from within yourselves; you will be greatly surprised by your findings. When you come to make a judgement, look to yourself before you judge. How many times do you believe you are correct, only to find that you are not? Before you judge, wait one moment; stand back and look, not at what you see, but look at your feelings; search within yourself. I know many of you will do this. You are learning, but your learning will take time. It will come over many years, over your whole lifetime. Your understanding of today may not be the understanding of tomorrow, for you will have passed through a new day. Tomorrow never holds the experiences of today. You will never re-live today.

You see around you human beings. You see the human aspect, because you are residing in a material vehicle, in a material environment. This environment is only temporary, it is not the true reality of life. It is the Spirit within and around you that is, in essence, the truth of all life. It is there that you will find your answers, and I stress: 'your' answers, not the answers belonging to other people, because you are on a pathway of growth, development and progress according to your own experiences. Many people will try to help you. They will try to guide you, to provide for you the experience of their own understanding. So they will say to you, "Read this book," or "Learn from this school or from this area of the country." You should turn to them and say, "Thank you, I welcome your interest in my pathway, but I will find the correct direction from within myself and from my own Companions from the World of Light."

Always walk slowly; do not tread on the delicate egg-shells, which are the feelings of others around you, for once damaged they cannot be mended. Learn to be wise, learn how to move around to avoid breaking the eggshells. Your words are important; do not hurt with your words. You will not be able to mend what you have broken, you will only be able to cover the damage. In my world, there is the opportunity to be beside those you prefer to be with. Here, your lessons are: to integrate with those you do not prefer to be with, learning to live together; to experience others' suffering and misfortune; to become tolerant of one another and to understand one another; to live beside your neighbour; and to support the people you know very little about.

All life has a Companion from my world. They will protect, guide and advise you. They will give to you their courage; their arm for you to lean upon when your pathway becomes very difficult. I am sure that there have been many occasions when your life has been very dark and difficult. At this time, it is for you to turn to the true essence of life for your assistance through the dark tunnel of education, because this is a dark tunnel. Many times when you are beginning to break through into a new learning process, all around you begins to lose its luminosity. So you tread in darkness, wondering where the tunnel will lead, where you will be moving to, and I am referring to your growth of the Spirit and your material pathway. "Why?" I believe you ask. I would say to you, it is because your material pathway is in conjunction with the growth of your Spirit. All is connected. All is intertwined together. You are here in this World of Matter to learn and to grow.

In my world, there are those who wish to talk. One day they will talk with you and with all your people. Life in your world is not restricted to your people. There are many forms of life. Learn to share and tolerate those around you, to be kind to those who do not have your understanding. One day they will know; they will see the light. Today, you have knowledge. Allow others their learning as you have had your learning. Your time here is surrounded with many problems in order for you to learn, to gain strength and develop in your own time. Allow others their time. Some of you will move faster than others. Do not compare yourselves to them, as there is no one here like another.

Your learning comes from your own experience. This is not the experience of another, for your life is not that of another. Very often, you believe you will gain knowledge and truth from the experiences of those around you, but this is not true. Each one of you is different. You are individual and, therefore, very special. Remember to be proud of yourselves. Very often, there will be times when you decide that you need a certain experience. You may believe this is your desire, but there are, in my world, many who stand beside you, who guide you in your progression. They will know that these experiences are important for you. From there, you must decide for yourselves your future. You may continue, or you may not, but for a growing number the decision is to continue.

This World of Matter is a classroom that is designed to provide certain lessons for you. So, your neighbour may be learning one subject and you may be learning another, but you are in the World of Matter, placed together side by side, but on two different pathways. So my people would advise you never to measure your own development, your own progress or your own life against that of another. Never compare. Never judge another. The only time that you are able to do this is if you have walked in the footsteps of that person, the footsteps of their life, and I, of course, refer to the 'Eternal Life'. No person would ever be able to do this, so never place yourselves above or below another. Always maintain equality.

Now, many do not fully understand the implications when a child of your world moves to my world. But within the vehicle of that child there may very well be a very progressed 'Being' indeed, and they will have chosen a short period of time in order to gain the necessary experiences to help them along their pathway. Their particular experiences in the World of Matter will be of benefit to them, and they will determine their forward progression by their actions and words within this world. So a child is not necessarily young Spirit. That Spirit will choose the vehicle that will be most suitable to their personal spiritual development.

When the parent comes to my world, at the termination of their time here, they will again meet with the child. They will meet with all whom they have loved and who have loved them, because this bond of energy, known as love, is unbreakable. So, when the time is right, the child will come to the parent and will stand and greet them upon the transition. The time of physical death to you is a time of birth to my people. It is a time of great celebration, where there is love, laughter, companionship and the imparting of information.

The garment that you now have around you only belongs to the World of Matter. Upon your transition to the World of Light you discard this garment, the vehicle (body). It is only pertinent for your manifestation within the 'schoolroom of life', here upon the planet. When you transcend to my world you regain your wholeness, so you will rejoin your 'Total Being', which may be well progressed in the eternal expression of life.

This is why my people always say to you, "Do not judge." The human being is very susceptible to judging all and everything. They say, "That person does not work hard enough. That person is in great pain. That person is lazy. This person over here has had a very difficult life, but that person has not." I would say to you, how do you know? This life here is not the beginning and it is not the end; it is only a small fraction of time within the eternal understanding, like a very small pebble within the oceans. So, it is true, when you come here to learn, you choose the implements of your learning. You choose your family, your vehicle and many of the obstacles within your life, because you know they will be of benefit to you. Not to you the human being, but to 'You' the Spirit.

Knowledge is of great importance. Never attempt to judge without knowledge. Very often, you are encouraged to read books. Many people will talk with you, but your knowledge comes from 'You', from within. You will know when it is right and when it is wrong. It is good to listen and read, but you will know. So, I encourage you to continue to learn and to gain experiences. I know many people within your world seek knowledge of my world. This knowledge, the truth of your searching, comes from within you. Many experiences within your lives, and the many pathways that you have travelled along, will grow within you. These experiences will include the knowledge of my world, but, all too often your people deny the inner knowledge and the inner understanding.

There may, at some time in the future, be the opportunity for 'You' the Spirit, to once again walk this world. The Spirit will return but will inhabit a different vehicle. The Spirit contains the memory of all lifetimes, so I inform you of 'Total Life', a life before now and a life in the future. The vehicle retains no memory, but the Spirit, the consciousness, retains total memory. Whilst you are here, each one of you is able to recall total memory. Use your experiences over many lifetimes, do not restrict yourselves to this time only.

My world is only one step from your world. At the time when each one of you places your foot over the threshold, the tool for your communication will be your mind. I encourage you to bring discipline and control to your mind, for you cannot hide your thinking in my world. So learn now; learn to control your thinking and take with you a polished tool. Continue to seek for knowledge and understanding, and you will grow strong. Very often there will be those who deny your knowledge. Know your own strength and remain with your strength. One day, your world and mine will join together.

I do not see ignorance in people, I only see the inability to unlock the door to the knowledge that is within all people.

Many people in your world do not see the possibility of life other than that of the human being. Their minds are closed. Sometimes, we will find a person who does not have the closed thinking of your people. We are able to transmit our thoughts to them and encourage the information about other life-forms, to be transmitted to others around them. Very often, with your people, the closed mind will damage the open mind. Words spoken with little thought may cause harm that is unseen. We are here in order to heal the damage that is done. We then encourage the single soul to tread the pathway of knowledge, understanding and wisdom.

When people are directed to environments where there is great knowledge of Spirit, they are then able to witness the presence of Spirit, to be informed of the true reality. Then it is for the individual to decide upon their pathway. Many will listen, many will not, but certain environments will provide the key for people. If they choose, they will then unlock the door to this knowledge. If they do not, they will continue to walk forwards.

I know the frustration within the very centre of persons who have great confidence in the presence of Spirit, when they do not see the reactions of people around them. What you do not see are the very, very small seeds that are being planted within the hearts and minds of people. You will only see when the flowers bloom. Very often these blooming flowers will not be within your vicinity, because they will have walked further along their pathway and they are now in another environment where they will be able to plant seeds of their own.

Sometimes, we know that the individual may desire to take control over their own progression, their own development. This may lead to turbulent waters, but the Companions, the friends from the 'worlds of Spirit and Light', will remain steadfast, like a rock. We will begin to bring around you a new understanding, a new comprehension of your circumstances, to try to re-direct you to the stability of the pathway so that you can gain your breath, your peace of mind, your balance and harmony. When this has been achieved, we will then take your hand and help you to continue your search.

Sometimes, my friends, it is not easy. Oh, no, definitely not. You may wonder why. It is because within each one of you there are the human qualities that are a part of your earthly being. This will require considerable mastery and will not always be successful, but we persevere because we love you and this is sometimes missing in life. All too quickly people around you will walk away when difficulties encompass you. Many find it hard to assist with the difficulties of other people, so they turn their back when often you need them, but my people, from the World of Light, will never turn their backs. Always we will stand with you, shoulder to shoulder, through turbulence, until you meet the warm shafts of sunshine that will inevitably come to you. But, my friend, always allow for time, because nothing can ever be achieved instantly.

When the waters of turbulence are around your shoulders, there needs to be time given to allow these waters to die away and for the balance and harmony to return. Many people will say, "Take my troubles away, bring me peace today." They will say, "I cannot walk another foot forwards, I am tired, I am drained." When the troubles persist, then they become disillusioned with the World of Spirit, but we are always there. We will place our arms around you to comfort, to love, to bring warmth when the cold is around you. We are also there to hold you back when you may run into the flames of fire. It is our desire to bring to you, all of the help that is within our power, but you need to grow; you need to develop as a 'Spirit being', not as a 'human being'.

To accomplish this task, it may be necessary for you to encounter boulders and pebbles upon your pathway. The development of your Spirit will show through when you try to face these obstacles. At this time we will stand and watch. It is all too easy to desire to interfere, but we cannot. How would you know of your progress if we interfered?

Many today, in your country, find in front of them a changing working environment. To some, this is traumatic because it is out of their control. Some may turn their anger upon those around them whom they love, causing distress amongst family and friends. Others will maintain their equilibrium and will begin to quietly seek alternatives with the support of family and friends. To quietly maintain the equilibrium shows the development of the Spirit.

Thoughtful Walk

Keep on walking, never stop
Turn your walk into a trot
Until you find a bench, to rest
There to plot tomorrow's test.

Gather strength and fortitude
Warm your soul, then say
The Sun is gathering altitude
It's time I was on my way.

Words from Companion of the Earth
Through the inspired writings of
Rev. Gayna Hilary Petit-Gittos (Tywane)

CHAPTER 8

Help from Spirit

Many, in your world today, believe that they can individually direct people to the source of information that will benefit them. Many people, also, believe in a unifying information, but I would disagree, because there is no unifying information for the individual development. Each one of you is separate from all others. Each one of you has received different experiences within your life, and I refer to your 'Total Life', so only you know your feelings, your knowledge and your experiences. Your Companions, also, will know the same, but people in this World of Matter are restricted with their vision, because of the vehicle in which they are encased. So, people try to judge the knowledge and actions of others without the full vision that is available to the Spirit, the Spirit without the vehicle.

I know that, many times during your lifetime, people will turn to you and comment upon your actions. They will attempt to make a decision upon whether or not you are correct in your actions, whether you are justified, whether or not the reason for your actions are plausible. I know also that, very often, you will be surprised by the comments, because you believed that your actions were substantially correct according to your understanding of the situation. Now, as a result of the comments made you begin to question, you begin to wonder and you begin to loose your self-esteem. You try to make adjustments to your actions according to the people around you, and then you become dissatisfied. You become concerned because your feelings alter, your emotions change. Now you begin to experience certain difficulties with yourself, with your actions and with the people around you who have made the comments. Some of you may understand yourselves and those around you, but others may become confused by this chain of events.

When you begin to experience the pathway of the Spirit, you begin to feel comfortable. You begin to feel that your movement forwards is flowing and light, but then the changes begin to occur for the reasons I have commented upon. You begin to be confused and you say, "Why am I confused? Why do I now alter my actions according to the comments of the people around me, and why do I feel these emotions?" I would venture to say to you that you have now begun to move slowly off the pathway of the Spirit. I, of course, refer to the pathway of your own Spirit not the Spirit of another. When you begin to move along the pathway according to your own understanding, your own development and progress, you feel good. When you move away, you begin to be confused. Always move according to your own understanding. Always move according to your emotions, according to your own thoughts, as those in my world will make effort to communicate with you via your thoughts, through your mind. My people will talk to you by using their thoughts and implanting their thoughts into your mind.

Your pathway will be discovered through your heart. Many people will try, and I emphasise 'try', to guide people along the pathway that they believe in, but only two people know your true destination. One person is your Companion from the World of Light. The other person is you. Discover your pathway by sitting and talking to these two very important people. Together you will be able to map your pathway. Your pathway is indeed planned before your arrival upon this World of Matter, but very often, without intent, the individual may go along an alternative route. So, there may come a time when it is necessary for you to sit and talk with yourself and your Companion so that the true pathway may once again be achieved.

So, your people, your Companions will make efforts to guide and advise you according to your own level of development, your own level of understanding. But, all too often, people around you try to enforce their own development upon you. They try to enforce their understanding and knowledge upon you and then they begin to judge. They judge you, they judge your actions, they judge your knowledge and your development, but they do not know your life. They do not know your experiences, and they do not know the emotions experienced by you as a result of your life experiences, so they are unable to compare themselves to you. I, of course, refer to your 'Total Life', I do not refer to your lifetime here. There is 'total life', 'total experience' and 'total emotion' embedded, for eternity, within 'You' the Spirit, not you the vehicle (the human being).

Confusion in your life occurs when you try to move forwards and you stumble. My people bring their influence around you and then you no longer stumble. But I do not say that you do not face troubles; you do, and these troubles are like boulders. Sometimes, they are really pebbles, but in your minds they become boulders. You are able to move around the boulders with the assistance of my people. With their knowledge and their vision, you are able to manipulate the difficulties placed before you. These difficulties are designed for you to grow and develop. Without problems you would not grow. You would not make effort to surmount these lessons, as there would be no lessons.

You are here in a 'schoolroom'. Your life is a school and you are requested to participate in the learning process. But all too often your people turn away, as they believe they are unable to succeed in their attempts to surmount the difficulties; but they do not know of the presence of my people.

When I walked your world, we did not sit ourselves upon hard structures; we placed ourselves in contact with Spirit: with the soil, with the grass. Then we knew that the power was a part of us. It is this world, which your people mistreat that is so important for you. It will provide for you ample nourishment to keep your vehicles (bodies) in motion. It has food and water so it can nourish you. She is your 'Mother'. She cares for you and yet your people take all they can from her. They are constantly taking and taking. They are constantly placing chemicals within the water, soil and atmosphere, depriving the planet of its opportunity to grow. She grows by providing all life-forms with nourishment. She gives to all without demand, without requirement for self-gratification. She gives to all life 'unconditional love'. Why do your people always place demands upon giving? "I will give this if you give me that. I will do that if I can have that and that and that." Always demands. Follow your world. Follow your 'Mother', she will help you.

Many, in your 'Spiritualist movement' today, forget the source of the information. They forget the Spirit. They forget the Great Spirit. Many believe that they are person-ally delivering the information, but they are not. It is delivered by the many Companions in my world, from the Great Spirit, through the material vehicle. It is delivered from the Great Spirit (God) - by Spirit (the Companions or Guides) - through Spirit (mediums/healers/inspired individuals) - to Spirit (all people/all life). Remember this and you will never fall upon the many pebbles that will be upon your pathway. When you gain trust, when you gain strength in the knowledge of this reality, then you will be able to face the pebbles at your feet and you will be able to remove them. They will be of no difficulty to you. The greater difficulty will be the immovable boulders that will come in front of you on occasions. When you reach a boulder utilise your knowledge, the knowledge from the Spirit. Use the wisdom that is available to you. Seek the advice and guidance of your Companions and move away. Do not allow fear to enter your heart, as this will cause you to struggle and struggle against the immovable boulder. Allow yourselves to flow, as the river flows to the Great Ocean.

Many tears are shed by your people as they struggle against the tide of opposition or change. Many try to remain static in their knowledge of who is around them. When you pull away from this security, then you will find the tunnel of darkness enters your life. But remember, this is the time of new lessons, of new direction that will bring to you greater and greater experiences, greater development of the truth of the Spirit. Allow yourselves to move in life. Allow yourselves to gain your strength from within.

At no time would my people ever aim to disturb you. They would never cause pain or suffering. If they were to push you, then they would indeed cause you disturbance. So they will never push you into making a move you do not feel ready for.

The only time that you will make a move is when you are strong in the knowledge of your move. When this is so, then you will move with ease, without tears or pain. Many people will not move, because they fear the removal of the security of love around them. The time when your move is correct will be when you are stable in thought, in heart and in soul. My people will stand beside you. They will feed to you their courage, their strength and their love, so that you will know that, whatever move you choose to make, it will be made within the cocoon of love.

Each one of you has abilities that enable you to connect

with the Companions in my world, to connect with the great 'Books' that exist, the 'Books of Time and Knowledge'. Within these 'Books' there is help for you. Your Companions have the ability to search these 'Books', to gain for you your direction.

Do not fight your way through life, but allow yourselves to be like the droplets of water that make the river grow as it reaches the source. The great ocean of Spirit is in front of you. I encourage you to learn to swim. My people will help you if you allow their presence around you. Each one of you has a Companion from my world, like me. They come to give you their hand in friendship. They come as strength and direction for you when your eyes are filled with tears. When there is pain in your heart, they will place their arms around you and give you comfort. They are there when many of your people here turn away. You are able to communicate with your Companions and feel their love, but very often, in your time of need, you will place around yourself an energy field that is tight. Everyone is energy and around you there is a field of energy. When that field expands, my people are able to stand within your energy, then you can feel. When it becomes difficult for you, your thoughts will shrink this field and my people stand outside, and when you cry they will cry with you. When your thoughts and heart reach out around you, your field of energy will expand, did you know? When your thoughts go to yourself then your field will shrink, did you know?

My people are standing with you now. They are making effort to guide you in the right direction. Do not be afraid of turning towards darkness because, sometimes, in order to know the light, you need to be shown the dark. At this time, in the darkness, your Companions will have their hand on your shoulder. They will give you the strength to go forwards and the love to support you.

Those in my world desire to assist you in your learning

process. They desire to encourage you and to bring their knowledge to aid you. In order for them to succeed, they require your co-operation. They desire for you to relinquish control. Not totally, as you need a degree of control to enable you to live in your world. The more you allow yourselves to be assisted by my people, the greater their assistance to you, as they will possess a greater knowledge that will help you in your life.

In this world, you are able to envisage a degree of success and failure according to your limited vision. Those in my world, who stand beside you, are able to see a greater degree of your life, so they are able to move you accordingly, around the corners of your path. Many times you may see a large boulder in front of you. You may desire to turn and move away as you feel your inability to deal with it. You do not have the confidence to confront it. Your Companion will know that you require the experience of the boulder to assist you in your continued development, so they will encourage you forwards. They will provide their arm for your assistance. They will provide their strength to assist you to gain the courage to go forwards. Your own control over your pathway will result in your desire to move backwards. The desire of your Companion will be contradictory to your desire. If you relinquish your own control and allow the Spirit to guide you, then you will grow strong.

I now seek from you a relinquishing of your control. My desire is for you to grow strong and to have confidence. The pathway in front of you will not be easy, as many times you will find that there is no light. At these times, you need to consider the Companions that walk with you. Allow them to show you the pathway that has been planned by you. There are times when you believe that you are alone. There will be times when you will see those around you, in your world, turn away. Despair will be felt by you. At these times you will grow, because you know of my people. They will move forwards and they will be your friends. You will never be alone, never, I always watch. You can never hide from me. I am placed here now, for you!

My people and I, very often, will stand by, and we will cry tears of sadness for you. We see your suffering and your pain, but many of you do not ask for help. You struggle by yourself and we want to help you. So, at this time we gather together in the World of Light and we centre our thoughts upon healing energy that will be transmitted to you. Then we pray to the Great Spirit for guidance and advice, for strength to fill us so that we can feed it to you. We give to you our love, but many of you turn away because of the indoctrination of your world, because of the false truth that has been given to you of the wickedness of my people. To us, this does not matter. What matters is that you, as a result, turn away, so we cannot feed to you the warmth and the love that you need.

Each one of you is a part of the Great Spirit, a part of the 'Whole'. So, available to you is the knowledge of the 'Whole'. The 'Whole Being' is all life; all that exists upon this planet, in your skies and in your universe. Life is not only what you see with your own eyes and hear with your own ears, but also what you do not see and hear. It is all within you. You, as individuals, have access the knowledge of the 'whole' though attunement with your own Spirit, with the Companions that stand beside you, and with the Great Spirit that is a part of all life. Turn your attention to the skies, for within your universe there is now an attempt to transmit information to your people. This information comes from 'Beings' that have greater knowledge than the human beings around you now.

My people, from the World of Light, are now making effort to bring education, knowledge and truth to your people. They are trying to show everyone the importance of respect for life, because there are changes that are taking place with your world. As a result of this, there are corre-sponding changes that are occurring to the life-forms that exist upon this World of Matter, changes to nature, to the animals, to the birds in your sky and to the human beings. Many of your people are now feeling these changes. They are beginning to sense a difference with the energy that is around them, but they do not fully understand the significance of these changes. So they search, as I have said, around them.

The pathway involving the work of Spirit may very often have many stones upon it and many changes of direction. These turns in your life appear to be sharp and darkness very often appears in front of you. Many times you will say, "I can go no further. I am afraid, for I do not see." When seeking the service of Spirit, we say to you, "The pathway is not easy." Many times you may say, "I fail," or "I do wrong." I would say to you that there is no failure, no wrongdoing, because you have tried. There is only failure when you do not try. There is always success in your attempt to further your knowledge and communication with those in my world. I admire you very much.

To go forwards without sight may cause great fear. I would say that many in my world stand beside you. They show you their hand, so that you may go together into the darkness. The one beside you will be your light, to guide you. There will be a time when you, too, will see the light. I say to you, "Grow strong, learn to know your Companion, learn to feel their personality and the union will grow strong."

I would always say that the greatest knowledge comes from your own Companions. The greatest direction, along the correct pathway for the individual, will come from the Companions and from within yourself, because you, too, are Spirit. You have the ability of reaching the Great Spirit. The Great Spirit is the creator of all life. You have the ability of reaching information from the 'Books of Time and

Knowledge' that exist within the World of Light. So, for all individuals, the direction is to go within and to go to the Companions, and through both of these avenues you will reach the Great Spirit.

There came a time, upon this world, when certain groups of people gained an everlasting understanding of the importance of harmony and balance between all that existed. I said 'everlasting', so now this knowledge and understanding is used by these people to bring education to the people now upon your world. This understanding has not been achieved by the people that inhabit the western areas of your world. It is an age-old understanding. Now, upon the request from the Great Spirit, the people who possess this understanding gather around your world. As they gather, they are able to access their memories of the time when they lived upon this planet. Many of them inhabited the ancient nations and are known as the Natives of America and the Orient.

I desire to bring information so that my people, in my world, can come to you and give you information, as beside each one of you there is a person like me. The people in my world, who stand beside you, are like you. They are human. They smile and laugh, but they are not restricted by the vehicle. They have vision that will assist you. They have many likes and dislikes, and they possess personality and character as you do. They do not change when they cross the threshold of physical death. Your family and friends in my world do not change, their vision just widens. When they talk to you, they talk to you with their mind. Listen to your thoughts, listen to your mind and you will hear them talk to you. Do not be afraid. They are not afraid of you.

So, for all of you, your pathway to development and knowledge, to a closer connection with your own Companions and with the Great Spirit, is through yourselves and through your Companions.

Many times, there are openings in your life when you need to be able to place yourself within the power of my people. When you are able to do so, then my people will be able to have a greater influence over you. But, very often it is difficult for you, as human beings, to allow the control of your vehicle, the control of your life, to be placed within the power of another. So, there will need to be times when you make effort to consciously remove yourself, so that my friends from the World of Light can show you their power, show you their influence.

Very often in your life, you believe that you can manipulate circumstances to suit your pathway. So you try to control; you try to guide yourself around many obstacles, around many corners and through situations that you are unaccustomed to. My people will watch; they will see your attempts. They will stand by and try to influence, but many human beings will build a barrier between themselves and my people, because, above all, they wish to remain in control. They wish to have power, to dominate. This is one of the difficulties of the World of Matter today, because the planet, which is Spirit, is itself taking away a large amount of control.

So, I come to you today to bring you the advice of my people. To encourage you to allow your friends, your Companions, to surround you with their power, like a cloak around your shoulders. I am aware of the difficulties that this will place for you, but the greatest learning comes through difficulties.

Very often, in the depths of the darkness comes the greatest trust in yourself and the Great Spirit. It is, very often, in the depths of this darkness that you make your greatest strides, your greatest development and your greatest progression. Many people are afraid of the dark, because they cannot see or control. You do not need to control. Allow the power to guide you. Allow yourselves to flow, as the river flows to its destination. Many people are like tributaries, flowing towards the river. When you join the river, then you join together as a greater power, a greater force that can achieve greater progress. You have the capacity to make great strides in the furtherance of the changes of this planet. You can all be a part of the great change that is now upon you. Do not feel alone. There are many such as you who are trying to use this power for the benefit of life.

Trust is a very strange phenomenon. It requires a release of yourself, and yet your people encourage you, and your society encourages you to be in control. So, from childhood you are trained to take control. You are discouraged from turning yourself, turning your life over to another being. Now, I come to you and I say to you to allow the release to occur. Allow 'You' to slip away from yourself. I am sure you are wondering why I say this. My people can see the future of your planet. They can feel, see and hear the very minute alterations of yourselves and the planet, so they know the direction that they wish to take you as individuals. But you, as human beings, cannot fully appreciate the changes taking place around you, because your vision is very limited by the existence of the human vehicle. So there will be a need for you to allow yourself to be directed; to be guided and sent along a certain pathway that will not only benefit you, but will also benefit the people around you and the planet.

No harm will come to you if you will only allow yourself to trust. 'Trust' is a very small word, but it is also very big, because it requires you to say to your Companions, "Take me. I give to you, me. I give to you, me not just for my benefit, but also for the benefit of the 'Whole'." This is because you are all learning to place yourself within the 'Whole' and to be, therefore, of benefit to the 'Whole'. Yes, indeed, you do have your lives to live here in this World of Matter. You have experiences that will be here for your benefit, but you, as individuals, are also of benefit to other beings, to other life-forms.

I know this can be very difficult for you because you wish to see. You wish to be fully aware of all the lessons around you, of all the experiences that come to you, because, if you cannot see, then you believe you are not learning. But you are, you know. You can learn from the unseen. There are very minute events happening around your world; events that do not, upon the surface, appear to be of any influence to you. Yet all the events, all the incidents of your world are of immeasurable influence and importance to you, because you belong to the 'Whole' and all that occurs to the 'Whole' will have relevance to you as Spirit.

Many abilities within you will rise. Many times, you may try to accomplish something and you may not be pleased with the results of your attempts, but these experiences will be necessary for your greater knowledge and awareness. You are the seed in the fertile soil that now begins to grow. The future of your world, now rests with you. Those in the higher realms of my world desire to see you growing strongly, so that the total evolution of the Spirit will be able to descend into your world. The Brothers of White Light will be seeking the transmittance of knowledge from you to the 'children of the Earth'. I believe that you are strong and capable of sustaining your truth, the truth of the Spirit, the truth of the universe. From you will come the peace of your people and the harmony in the countries around your world.

There are many from the World of Light who come to assist, who come to help your people, your world. There are great minds from the universe gathering around your world, who are trying to feed information to the World of Light. This information is currently being banked in the World of Light. From the bank, this information will be filtered through to the World of Matter. It will be delivered by the Companions that are beside you. The World of Light requires the power of the 'white light' in order to deliver the assistance that you need, but many are turning off this 'white light'. Many are turning their backs upon the presence of Spirit, so there are areas of your world that are going into darkness. People are preferring the darker energy of aggression, violence and material power. They are desiring control, so they destroy the environment and the animals. They destroy the human beings in order to gain a greater and greater power for themselves, a power of the World of Matter. This darker power is a slower vibrating energy.

The power of the 'white light' is a finer energy, and your world is currently trying to move into the finer energy. But there are many people who are trying to pull away. They are trying to restrict this increase of energy, because with it will come a different lifestyle for all the inhabitants of the World of Matter.

So, I now take this opportunity to bring to you the knowledge that it is not sufficient for you to only sit and learn, but it is necessary for you, in the process of learning, to allow the greater power to envelop you. You are learning not only for your own benefit, but also for the benefit of the 'Whole', because your individual learning will, when returning to the World of Light, be placed into the basin of knowledge from which Spirit will drink.

Those beside you, from my world, desire to assist you, desire to bring you knowledge. Turn to your Companions, like Tywane turns to me. I provide for her my strength and encouragement. I also give to her my love. Those beside you, from my world, desire to give to you their advice, guidance and love. The Brothers of White Light desire to encourage the evolutionary process of your people. They try to find people who will assist them in their desire to bring harmony and peace to your troubled countries. You are now a part of an army of knowledge, to fight the ignorant and to inform your world of this desire of the Brothers of White Light. I respect 'The Brothers' and I also respect you.

CHAPTER 9

Communicating with Spirit

There is a world beyond the veil that separates the World of Spirit from the World of Matter. Those who learn, those who search with their mind are able to penetrate this veil and so begin to see the many, many people who reside in this world. But there are still those, and their numbers are great, who turn away from this information, from this knowledge, from this reality. They turn away because of fear and ignorance.

Every human being has the ability to communicate with my people, if they choose to do so, because of one very significant factor, they are Spirit. I am Spirit and Tywane is Spirit. Spirit communicates through Spirit to Spirit. So, all living creatures upon this planet can communicate, because they are communicating with a world of Spirit.

The essence of every living being is the power of love. This light pulsates through every being. It is very forceful and often misunderstood by the human being. I do not refer to the crude understanding of love known to the human being. I refer to something that is very deep, very meaningful and bonding that will bring two or more people together and will be everlasting. It is very beautiful, powerful, strong and pulsating. It is there throughout the universe. It is within all of existence. It is seen as light, and light can be seen in many varying shades of colour. The human being, if sensitive, can register this power. I am today communicating through this power. It is this force that allows me to come close to this World of Matter, in order for me to communicate information from my world to your world that will be of significance to your people.

Very often, people are afraid. They fear the negative element imposing upon them. But my people and my World of Light care about your world. We love your world. A great compassion is felt by us, for the many hardships that are encountered by your people. We are always standing upon your shoulders, waiting to help with information and support, to allow you as an individual to go through the many complicated lessons that exist within life upon this planet.

We stand and watch, and we cry as you cry. We try to enfold you in our arms, and provide support and warmth when the cold winds blow and when the rain falls upon your shoulders. We wait and wait, then, when you turn your attention and head towards the sky and shout for help, we are there and we help. We then come forwards into your energy and we are able to move you, in order for you to find answers to your problems. But fear and ignorance are, very often, the barriers between our worlds. This is why I come. This is why I try to educate, try to gently open the petals within your mind to the true existence of the World of Spirit.

Those who believe that this World of Matter is the only form of existence, their minds are closed and we cannot force these petals open. If we tried, then the individual would become burnt by the power of the Sun that shines down. As the rose in the garden needs time for each delicate petal to open, so the mind of the human being also needs time. Then they will slowly become accustomed to this very, very powerful source, this Sun that brings warmth and friendship when human friendship disappears.

When an individual begins to open their heart, like a rose beginning to blossom and opening its petals, a degree of sensitivity begins to grow within that human being. This sensitivity needs to be understood, because the words spoken by people are no longer words; they are threads of energy. These threads vibrate, and this vibration begins to affect the individual who is on the receiving end of this energy. People around do not know this, but the growing, developing 'sensitive' begins to recognise and learn about this energy. When the harshness begins to penetrate, there is a desire for the rose to begin to close the petals and withdraw, but I would say to you, do not do this. Allow the petals to remain open and around this rose a new energy will be built by my people. It will be built by the Companions who stand at your side, who try to advise and direct, to shine a light so that, in the development of the rose, the pathway ahead gains clarity.

Many young people today are beginning to learn, beginning to make effort, and yet they are being constantly turned away by the misunderstanding, selfishness and greed of the older populations. No longer are there the men and women of wisdom, of understanding and compassion. Instead, there is the requirement for greater physical wealth (the bigger car, the large money account) or positions of power and control (control over life, whether they be human beings or animals, trees, rivers or the flowers that grow upon your land; all of this is Spirit, all of this is 'You').

Each one of you, each human being upon this planet, all of the animals, all of nature - the rivers, the trees, the soil beneath your foot, the air that you breathe - all of this is Spirit. All of this comes from the Great Spirit. All life are, therefore, brothers and sisters. No longer is your world your neighbour or your family; your world is the whole planet. The whole planet requires your respect, your help and consideration, because all belongs to the 'Whole'. All aspects of Spirit belong to the Great Spirit, to the 'Whole'. So, you are no longer considering another person, you are considering yourself by your consideration of that person, because you are an element of the 'Whole'.

So, now it is for you to make effort to encompass not only what you do not see, hear, and feel, but also what you do see, hear and feel. It is around you. The planets within your universe are there, like your planet, for the forwarding of the eternal life of Spirit. There are many life-forms that are gathering around your planet now, to bring to you assistance and guidance, because your world is changing, your people are changing, but the change is in differing areas. It is now that your world needs to move forwards, along the pathway for growth and development, but your people are very comfortable with the element of negativity upon this planet. It allows them to express the elements of greed and power. So there is a pulling of energy between the planet that wishes to go forwards, and the human beings who wish to stay. So you see outbreaks of violence within your own populations and within the environment.

We come to you now to say, "Let go and allow us to take you and your world forwards." If you do so, you will see the peace, the tranquillity, the harmony and balance. It will all be around you, and you will be able to connect with your very being, to connect with Spirit, to connect with the Great Spirit. Your world will lighten; the beauty will, once again, come within all lives, and this is important, for darkness within the life of one also belongs to all, because you are all a part of the 'One'.

So you are here, today, desiring to learn about a world that you do not normally see, hear or feel. You wish to discover the undiscoverable, and yet it is within you all of the time. It is around you all of the time. You are very often too busy to communicate, to allow yourself to become in tune with your own reality. Your own reality is the energy that belongs to you, because all Spirit, all life is energy that will vibrate at a particular speed.

When 'You' unite with the material vehicle in which you

now inhabit, your own energy is reduced in vibration, to allow you to communicate with many 'Spirit beings' from different areas of the eternal life. When you return to my world, to the World of Light, you will then reside with 'beings' of your own particular expression, your own particular development and progression. In order to expand the qualities of Spirit, you need to encounter all differing Spirit forms, so you come to this world, known to you as Earth, in order for you to do so. When you encounter other life-forms, it is then for you to bring forwards, predominantly, all of the qualities of the Spirit. You are required to manifest the perfection of Spirit. These qualities are patience, tolerance, understanding, compassion and love, but how many of your people forget all of these? How many of your people bring forwards the many elements of negativity? How many do you see, do you hear, who bring forwards greed, jealousy, anger and hatred? All of these are easy to express, but it is not so easy to express the perfection of Spirit.

When my people came to your people, over one hundred years ago, there was very little knowledge of my World of Light. So there was a need for certain persons, amongst the many human beings, to be utilised, in order for the truth and the knowledge of my world to be spread to all people. Very slowly, there became an awakening. Now, amongst the people of your world, there is an understanding that is allowed to manifest. There is an understanding that my World of Light exists, that you are not here for a set period of time, and that there is indeed eternal existence, eternal progression available to all life. So today we have people who understand this.

There was a time when my colleagues were able to talk to many hundreds of people, at a time when your world was in turmoil. Then, the people flocked to my colleagues, desiring the knowledge that their people, their relatives, their family and friends continued to exist. But, very slowly, the individuals within your 'Spiritualist movement' (and I talk of your 'movement' and not my people) have placed barriers (the walls of regulations) around my people; around their ability to move amongst your people and to talk to them as my colleagues talked many hundreds of years ago. Now, the Brothers of White Light have chosen to come again to your people, to bring them together, to unite those who are divided. My people now need to inform all people that there should be no fear. When you are engaging with the World of Light you are bringing into your life love.

My people, from the World of Light, have been communicating with human beings, through thought, for many, many years. Very often, it is in an unconscious manner. We work very subtly, because a shock occurring in the mind of the human being can very often close the enquiring mind. So, to bring information and instruction to your people, there is need for my people to work very carefully, very gently, bringing a thought here and a picture there, so slowly building a structure within the mind of the individual without them consciously realising this. Many people think that they themselves are gaining these ideas, these concepts, but the information is in actual fact coming from my people. Thought is a very delicate process, and it is through thought that my people communicate. In listening to your thoughts, you are very often listening to the people in the World of Light.

I would ask you for one moment to stop and to listen. Listen to the quiet, to the silence. Let your mind acknowledge stillness, peace and harmony. Your planet requires this peace. The thoughts of the human beings require this peace, but all too often your minds are very busy, very active with contemplations of the daily events within your life. So, many of your people ask me, "Why do I not hear Spirit? Why can I not feel Spirit?" I would say, always the minds of the people are too busy, too active to properly connect with my people from the World of Light.

Within your daily activities, always there is required a short period of time when you are able to sit and commune with Spirit: commune with yourself (Spirit), and with my people (who are Spirit). You are residing within the boundaries of the material schoolroom of life. You are here to engage with certain experiences that will help you to learn, help you to grow and develop - and I do not refer to you the human being, I refer to 'You' the Spirit - but many of your people do not give themselves time.

I am aware that many human beings today do give themselves thought but not time. I am referring to the proverbial 'I'. I need this. I want that. I will go there. I do not want. So, they give themselves this thought, but they do not give themselves, their true identity the required period for peace, tranquillity, harmony and balance. All of this is required by the life-forms upon your World of Matter.

Your world today moves too quickly. It is always concerned with output, with the building of finances that are far beyond the needs of the people involved. It is no longer concerned with the cares and the needs of individuals. People do not stop to look or listen. They are too busy. There is, for the benefit of the Spirit, a need for a calm, peaceful movement through life. There will be many obstacles that will disturb this peace and balance that you will try to gain. This is where the strength and discipline comes to you, in order for you to outstretch your arms and encompass these difficulties and obstacles and remain at one with life. When you can achieve this, then you will no longer cause disturbance to people around you. You will not cause them harm, pain or suffering. In one's haste, one will forget the needs of others. In that moment of forgetting, you have caused pain. You have caused harm, because you are forgetting the importance of another life form. You are not giving respect to another individual.

Your world is fast and noisy. Many disturbances are within the atmosphere, with people talking and creating great noise. For the Spirit, this can be disturbing. The World of Light is a very calm environment, very peaceful and still. The Spirit will learn many things in the World of Matter. Many experiences will come to help to teach you. One experience, that many of you do not see, is the experience of being in a disturbing environment. It is for each one of you to learn to regain the stillness of the environment of the World of Light, for you to gain a peace within yourself.

Many of your people will turn and say, "I have no time. I cannot sit for long, because I need to do this or I need to do that. I need to be busy." People fail to realise that the Spirit, also, is in need of certain requirements. There is a discipline in being able to sit without movement, without disturbance within yourself. This discipline is acquired over a period of time. At the beginning, you may feel uncomfortable. Your vehicle may cause you disturbance. Your mind, also, may cause you disturbance, because within your mind there will be thoughts that will create within you a violation of your stillness. It is for you to learn how to connect with the Spirit within you.

Your breathing is primarily important. Many people do not breathe correctly. They create a disturbance of their own physical being by their inability to control the breath of life. As you centre your attention upon this level of breathing, you are quietening your mind, because all thought will go to your breathing. You will eliminate your shopping, cooking, cleaning and your work. Eventually, when you sit and breathe from your stomach (solar plexus), you will move aside the thoughts of your physical environment and you will begin to bring forwards thoughts about the welfare of your physical vehicle.

Many people create their own physical ailments, because

they input into their vehicle unnatural substances that will only cause harm to the vehicle. The vehicle is energy. It is water and chemicals. When you begin to alter these elements, by addition of other elements, then you begin to disturb the peace of the vehicle. The vehicle is designed to allow 'You' the Spirit, to manifest in an alien environment. It is perfect for you. It is only you that creates the imperfection. So it is important for you to eat and drink correctly during your lifetime. As you contemplate upon this change for yourself, you will be purifying the thoughts within your mind. No longer will you have time to think about the most dreadful colour of the dress belonging to the woman down the road. You will not be able to be disturbed by the new car of the man over the road. Noisy children who run in your road will not disturb you. You will be bringing your thoughts together, and you will be centralizing upon the necessity and not the wants and desires of yourself (i.e. the want for the better car, or the desire for the children to be removed from your road because they disturb you).

Many of you breathe from your chest. You should all breathe from your stomach. This is where the action of the vehicle takes place, because of the build of the body. There is a mechanism here that will inflate and deflate the lungs within you. By restricting your breathing just to the chest, you are not utilising the mechanism that is designed for your breathing.

By slowing down your breathing, you are bringing a calm to your energy. The more peaceful you become, the closer the Companions around you can come also. They reside in an environment of peaceful energy. In order for them to gain a close connection to you, they require a peaceful energy. If you have a disturbance with your energy, because of your vehicle, because of your emotions or your thoughts, then this creates a problem for the Companions. When you sit quietly, they come close to you. At this time, you are also able to feel your own Spirit. You are able to feel 'yourself'; not the human being that is the façade, but the reality, the truth that is within and around you. This true self is a finer version of you. It is a more powerful element to the 'Being' that you are. It is more than what you see in your mirror.

As you breathe slowly and deeply, with calmness and peace, so you will begin to move slowly. You will stop rushing through your life. You will stop allowing life to shoot by without you seeing, feeling or hearing. As you move slower, you will then begin to see the beauties of life around you. You will see the blade of grass that is green and sparkling with dew, the flower that has opened and shows colour and perfume, and the sky that changes from blue to grey and from grey to blue. You will see the stars twinkling in the sky, the smiles upon the faces of other people, animals playing gleefully around your feet, and you will see the rain and the Sun. You will begin to see life.

So, to begin with, it is important to gain a peace and a balance with yourselves, respect life, respect yourselves and those within your company, and gain freedom from the physical restrictions of the human being. All of this causes disturbance. For you to be totally free and at one with life, you need to be able to combat all of these disturbances. When you have achieved this 'at-one-ment', then you will be free to connect with the wiser beings from the World of Light. They, in return, will bring around you a great power that will help you to surge through life and to regain confidence in yourself and in people.

Many people will accept Spirit, but they only accept Spirit outside of themselves. People are taught to communicate with Spirit in the World of Light, but they are not taught to connect with themselves. So you need to learn about all of Spirit. You need to learn about my people; about your people, here in the World of Matter; about the planet that supports you and about the other life-forms that exist around you. All of this is important, because you are then learning about and connecting with the Great Spirit, with the source of life. If you only connect with one single element of Spirit, then you will never be totally in balance and harmony with life.

You will be able to communicate with Spirit by talking to the land, the trees, the river and the soil. By talking to the wind, to the Sun and to the planets, you will be talking to Spirit. Many people dismiss the 'Spirit of nature'. They do not believe in the existence of Spirit in these areas. Talking to the Spirit of nature is as important as talking to me or you. Utilise your thoughts, utilise your voice, and you will build a power between yourself and the Spirit of the World of Matter.

Very often, within my world there are those who say, "I can see people in the World of Matter. I can see their appreciation for us." They say, "I desire to communicate with these people, but I do not know how. Show me." There are those, like me, who will take these people to areas of your country where we know your meetings take place, and we will show them the attempts that people make, in your groups, to communicate with my world. Very often, those in my world stand by without any talking taking place between the two worlds, and their attempts to talk with you become frustrating, for the knowledge of communication does not exist in your world.

My people use their minds and their thoughts to communicate. They communicate to you through the Spirit. Mind communicates to Mind. Spirit talks to Spirit. I am able to communicate by utilising the energy within and around the vehicle of Tywane. She allows me to come and talk to you. But many of my people will stand beside you, and they will guide and advise you by implanting their thoughts within your mind. So, your actions belong to you, your emotions belong to you and your thoughts belong to my people. We talk to you through your mind. Very often, you will search for communication with your physical eyes and ears, but this is not the truth. Search for communication through thoughts, and you will succeed. Do not turn and deny your ability to think, for you deny the truth.

There are those who say to themselves, "I am in control. I make the decisions regarding my life." To a degree, this is true. To a larger degree, it is not. In my world, there are your friends and family, who stand beside you, who assist with your pathway of life. Very often, they will watch your suffering and pain and be unable to help, for you do not turn for their assistance. By all means control your lives, but do not deny those beside you, for they are there to help and to guide. There are those beside you who seek to teach you. I say to you, talk with them. Seek their knowledge through your mind, for they will talk in your mind.

Many people in your world place great emphasis upon being titled with names or position. This is a means of identification within the World of Matter. When you return to the World of Light you are seen by your results. You are known by your thoughts, by your emanation of light, so there is no real need for titles. When my people come to walk beside you for your time here, they will remember their last life upon this World of Matter and into their mind will come the title that they were known by in this world. There are people who are able to hear this title and there are people who cannot. I would also state that, for some people there will be Companions who have no association with this World of Matter and for them there will be no title. Do not be concerned about this. If you are able to feel the presence of your friend in my world, then you are knowing of this person. Their guidance, their advice and their strength, for you, will be equally as strong as for those who know the title of their Companion.

Many people go through their lifetime here without touching life. Around all of you, there are numerous life-forms that are all interacting with each other. Now you will begin to learn how to interact yourself, so gaining a greater power; the greater power of the 'Whole' and not just a part, or the individual.

Each one of you is within the World of Matter in order to learn how to evolve with the 'Whole'. So the 'school-room' (the World of Matter) allows you to gain a certain understanding, to assist you to learn how to become a part of the 'Whole'. I, of course, refer to the whole of life, to the Great Spirit. So, over time, you will not only be learning how to interact with life in the World of Matter, but also how to participate in the communication of life that exists around the planet. So my people will be turning your attention to the sky. There are larger numbers of life-forms that exist within that area than there are here. This World of Matter is merely a small pebble in the greater ocean. I would appreciate you remembering this point, because it will then allow you to fully understand the true significance of the human being.

Many of your people believe implicitly that the human being is the most predominant and important aspect of the World of Matter, so they believe they can override all life, but they cannot. There are greater forces and a greater power that has overall control over existence. This power is the Great Spirit. Remember, the Great Spirit is not a person, not a being, but a 'Power' that infiltrates and permeates the whole of your universe, the whole of many, many universes, and many planets in many different vibrations of energy. This is why you need to learn the importance of energy.

There are people who cannot allow their minds to expand sufficiently to encompass the greater numbers of vibrating planes of energy, so they restrict themselves. I wish to encourage you to push your minds wider and wider, as the wider the mind, the wider the channel. Your mind is Spirit. You will be the channel for the 'greater Spirit' through the capacity of the mind. When this is accomplished, then the 'Minds' from your universe will be able to come closer to this planet.

Allow yourselves to see and to listen. Allow yourselves to feel the power that is around you, to feel the energy of your Companions. Allow them to move you. Become accustomed to being told where to go, what to see. Very slowly, by your release of control over yourself, you will be gaining a greater experience of life, and I am referring to 'You' the Spirit. By releasing individual control, you will be pushing away the barriers of matter, so bringing to you a greater pleasure than is currently available. The barriers and restrictions of matter prevent many of your people from gaining a greater experience from life. Allow yourselves to remain positive. All that occurs to you will be positive, even though you may see great negativity. Try to reverse your sight and you will then see the broader pathway opening up in front of you.

Communication is not easy, but we will go on knowing the truth. We will go forward with you into the darkness, because I know that in the darkness, for each one of you, there is light, a shining star. Find the light and follow it. Many times, the difficulty appears too great, but a shared difficulty will bring you a lesser burden. I say to you to search and find your truth of my world. Search within yourselves. Within you there is knowledge and understanding. Listen to your thoughts. Very often, when times become hard you close your mind to my world. At these times, my people stand beside you and they watch and wait, for only when you ask for their help are they able to oblige.

Within your world, many troubles occur. Many people are in conflict with each other. Your world is now disturbed. The life on your world has also become disturbed. At these times, my people come very close to you, to bring their strength and encouragement, for they know of your troubles. Very often, they will try to guide you, but many of you often deny their efforts. During the denial, you continue to seek the knowledge and understanding of my world. In times of quiet, my people are able to influence you. Consider how many times you are quiet, how many times do you stop and make your mind peaceful.

People who stand as teachers of the abilities of the Spirit consider only those abilities, they forget the importance of the Great Spirit. They forget that the most important aspect of the learning, is the growth and development of the Spirit. Such growth and development comes from the individual, by bringing forwards to all life the qualities of the Spirit: patience, kindness, tolerance and compassion. All of these are the jewels of the Spirit and will be taken with you to the World of Light.

I bring to you the love of my people. They desire for your people to see the reality of Spirit not just to be told, not just to read your books, but also to see and hear the truth. The controls, regulations and barriers that are placed around the 'Spiritualist movement' are allowing the people in the World of Matter (channels/mediums) to become predominant. There is a forgetting of the source of the information.

The expression of love is the epitome of life. Your people today forget to love. They forget the elements of love. So, there is no longer forgiveness, tolerance, understanding and patience. All of this is being lost in the single-minded direction of the human being. Today, you reside in the world of the machine. The introduction of the machine has brought about a speed of existence. All that is achieved is expected now, because your machines can produce now, so a mechanisation of the human being is taking place. Where are the qualities of the Spirit? The Spirit does not show its strength now. You will only see your progress as time in your world moves on. Sometimes, you will only see your progress when you travel back to the World of Light, when you pass through the veil between the World of Matter and the World of Light. When you reach this point, then all that has been and all that is will be shown to you.

I bring you the reality, the truth of the existence of Spirit, Spirit being the primary element and the human being the secondary element. I bring to you the importance of the qualities of the Spirit. It is for you to manifest these qualities, the reality of Spirit, through the material vehicle during your travels along your pathway.

CHAPTER 10

Joining the Healing Spirits

Many of you are now searching along your own pathway, to find an avenue through which you can utilise your abilities of communicating with my people. You search through books, or talk to people whom you believe have the knowledge that you are seeking, but fail at every turn to find the correct advice and guidance that will assist you in your union with my people.

For those who begin the walk towards the opening of the mind and the heart to the eternal existence of all life, the rainbows of colour begin to shine. They begin to feed and direct the individual along a pathway that will bring to them many experiences and many people, where information and energy can be transmitted. It is for these people to begin to open up and to talk to those around them. For some this is difficult, I know, because they fear the many harsh words of those around them, the criticisms and degradation. They fear the dismissal by people who themselves do not know but who choose to judge, who choose to condemn another for a differing belief, a different understanding of life.

Very often, with people in your world, there is a forgetfulness to raise their voices to the Great Spirit. Within your world today there is sorrow, pain and suffering caused by your people to your people. Too often, there is forgetfulness to the needs of the people, to the requirements of the Spirit that is within all life. The human beings today believe themselves to be the centre of all existence, and that all life around them is for the control and power of the human being. This is not so. As I have explained many times, each one of you comes from the same source, from the Great Spirit, and all life originates from the Great Spirit. So the animals, trees, water and soil, all of this being life, comes from the Great Spirit, so you are all brothers and sisters. You are all, also, a part of the 'Whole'. When pain and suffering is caused to one single life form then this pain and suffering is caused to all life.

My people now come to you all, to encourage you to bring about a change within your world. I say your world, not your country, because today your world is your home. Not one country, not one town, not one street, but a whole planet; the planet known to you as Earth. Each one of you here has the capability of making change that will affect the whole of your World of Matter. By your thoughts and your actions will there be built a great power, the power of the 'white light' that will be seen and utilised by my people.

Thought is energy. Collective thinking is power. When centred upon the good, it is a very powerful light and to the light will come many, many beings from the universe and from the worlds of light and colour. Energy creates colour, and vibrations of colour have effects upon all that is around. The most powerful is the 'white' light. The healing energy of the white light needs now to be centred upon areas of your world. There are those, in your universe, who have knowledge of the use of this power. They are interested in your application of this energy, so, when you centre your attention upon this light, become mindful of their influence.

You have the capability, within your hearts, to bring love to your world. Many of your people have forgotten the power of love! So I bring to you my own love and the love of the Brothers. A great power is now being built, under the guidance and advice of my people from the World of Light. We will bring to your people the knowledge and reality of my world.

Many people believe that they know the truth, but they promote very different information to the truth. We will attempt to eliminate the negative aspects of anger, jealousy, greed, control and power, which manifest within your world. There needs to be, instead, a building of brotherhood between your people and all life within your World of Matter and within the World of Light.

This brotherhood will result in the building of an arc of light around your world, from centres that are being instigated by my people. This will build a power of peace, tranquillity and harmony between yourselves; between you and nature; and between you, nature and the planets within your universe. This is because, gathering now, around your planet, are great minds from your universe who have knowledge of the development of the power of love to impart to you all!

There are many differing experiences in the area of the healing capacity. Many abilities are available to my people. Very often, in the years gone by, emphasis was placed upon the visual effects of the healing process, so it was necessary for my people to deliver a certain method of healing. The conditions for this method were appropriate under the energy circumstances of the planet, but your world now is changing. The energy belonging to the World of Matter is gaining a finer and finer vibration, so there is a need to refine the healing process.

There are times when alterations are required to the etheric blanket of the individual. When these alterations have been made, then there will be a change to the physical vehicle. Sometimes, there are changes made to the vehicle that do not reach the Spirit, that do not reach the etheric blanket, so these changes to the vehicle do not totally create a healing process. My people have the ability to utilise certain persons in order to achieve this connection through to the Spirit. At this point, those with knowledge of medicine, from my world, will make their adjustments. When the full waking occurs to the individual, they very soon become aware of changes that have taken place, not to their vehicle, but to their very being.

Many people reminisce about the physical abilities of the persons in your world during time gone by. Many, today, make effort to re-enact these very striking abilities, and indeed there are individuals who are still capable of doing so, but constantly you pull away to the past when my people are trying to push you forwards. Many will remain with the past, but I know that there are greater numbers who will go to the future. The future will bring greater healing capabilities, greater philosophy, and greater truth about the World of Light. The ability of physical healing was brought to enable people to see the capabilities of the World of Light, but they chose to see in a very physical fashion. Now it is time for you all to look with the eyes of Spirit.

I like to look upon people in their true image, the image of Spirit. You are all very beautiful. You are merely encased in matter that is fashioned according to the World of Matter. Your vehicles are not the truth. They are not you. You are Spirit. You are bright as light. You have love in your heart. I see each one of you in different colours, each radiating with individual beauty. I like to look at life.

There is a need for healing energy to now permeate the whole of your world, to bring about a change that is now trying to manifest, a change with the energy of your planet, so allowing a faster vibration to take place. Remember, you are a part of this change. You are a very important aspect of the universal alteration occurring around you now. There is a great need for you to acknowledge and accept this alteration, a need for you to take an active role in the forming of a bond between all life.

Your world is going through a great change. There are many in my world who are currently looking to your world, to your people, to try to find a way to help all life. Many of you are beginning to feel an alteration with yourselves and with your environment. But we are very aware that many of your people do not fully understand, or appreciate these very subtle alterations to the energy within and around your world. So we feel a great need to assist you, to bring to your people knowledge and experience that will aid and assist them in understanding the fine processes taking place with your planet.

Your people are now divided into two groups. There are those who are seeking to understand, who know of the importance of life and desire a greater knowledge and awareness, because they wish to assist in the progress of the human beings and of the World of Matter.

There are also, those who are turning away, turning away from knowledge, from the truth and reality of life. They are saying, "No" to education, because they are comfortable with the current position of this world. They are engrossed within the benefits of the material environment. Many people seek only their own gratification of material wealth. They try very hard to gain many possessions for themselves and for the people in their immediate environment. They say, "No" to the predominance of life. They do not believe in the reality of Spirit.

Your people forget the primary element of the Spirit, which is 'Love'. They forget the importance of compassion, kindness, tolerance and understanding. They are forgetting to love.

Your world, all life, grows as a result of the input of love, but many people today, because of the expansion of the age of technology, believe that growth takes place as a result of the input of knowledge. I would say to you, the greatest growth, development and progression occurs when you place knowledge with experience and input both into the Spirit, allowing the Spirit to absorb all and to bring forwards the element of love.

All life is created by the impact of love. Life is not created by a machine, or by the absorption of facts and figures. Life is created by, and grows and develops through, the transmittance of energy. The greatest energy comes from the emotion of love. Your World of Matter is now making effort to progress, to move to a time when the energy within and around the planet gains a finer and finer vibration. This is aided and assisted by the input, from the life-forms upon the World of Matter, of the energy of love.

Too often, people will turn away from those who are in need. They turn away from those who are starving, who are in deprivation and poverty, because many today believe in individuals gaining, for themselves, success. Your people, the governments of the world, are expecting individual success. There are not many people today who place emphasis upon the success of the 'Whole'.

Over many years, the human beings' capabilities of manipulating matter have expanded and expanded, to the point, now, where those people who understand science and medicine believe themselves capable of controlling life. They fail to realise that they are not controlling life; they are merely manipulating and constructing matter. But these people believe matter is indeed life. So now they believe in the total control of all that exists. This is why you now have circumstances where individuals, within certain areas, possess great power and control, and other individuals around them alter their approach to these people. This is not good, because there will come a time when other forms of life, different to the human being, will desire their own strength and control, and their will be altercation between the two.

Your world, today, now sees a removal of respect for all life, because, in order to produce artificially grown elements of the human vehicle, there is harm being caused to animals. There is no respect. There is no regard for the life that is being used. How would you like to be used for another being? To be used is to remove respect for the individual. All individuals have a respect within themselves. This is most important for the growth and development of the Spirit.

Each one of you has your own power to live your life in the manner that you have desired. When people begin to use an individual, this power begins to be moved, transmitted from you to the user, so your own self-respect begins to crumble. You begin to consider yourself less and less. Many people within the family environment use each other. There should not be the use of another life. There should always be co-operation and a respect and love for all life.

Many of your people of science and medicine use the animals in order to experiment. So the power belonging to the animals is transmitted to the human being, so lowering the self-respect of the animal. How do you think the animal, in this experiment, is feeling? Try to place yourselves as the animal. It has been removed from its natural habitat. It is being caged, and its vehicle is being altered without its permission. The animal is being humiliated. I am sure you would not like to be humiliated. This is for the benefit of the cosmetic vision of the human being. It is also for the benefit of the human being in areas that have not been chosen by the Spirit of the human being.

All life comes from the one source, from the Great Spirit, the creator of life. All life, when placed together, is a 'Whole'. The progress of the 'Whole' takes precedence over the individual, because all life is eternal, moving through growth, moving through eternity together. When individuals hang back, then the 'Whole' makes an effort to encourage these life-forms, so that all life gains the benefit of the light, the power and the energy; gains the benefit of true unconditional love.

There are children, in your world today, who do not

know the true meaning of love. Many children starve. Many are lonely, without supervision to assist them in knowing all aspects of the Spirit. So my people are now trying to come closer and closer to the people of your world, to bring their knowledge, to give guidance and advice.

Your planet and all that exists upon and around your planet, is Spirit. As Spirit, your planet is very aware of the requirement for it to move to a finer vibration of energy, so it is making an effort. Unfortunately, there are many human beings who are aware of the changes taking place, and they do not desire this movement. All human beings, being Spirit, are themselves energy. Now we find the energy of the planet battling against the energy of the human being, so causing a pulling of an energy that is between the two forces. As a result, there is an increase in the energy pressure. This increase is building to create a situation that will pull the planet forwards. Many of the human beings are feeling this energy, and it is stimulating aggression and violence within the populations.

The human being seems to believe that the only way to achieve greater power is to create weapons of great destruction, so that one nation can control another. So they are persisting in the desire to rule all life. In doing so, they are causing great harm to the marine life, to the planet and to each other, because, in trying to perfect weapons of great destruction within the great oceans of your world, they are causing human being to fight with human being. They are destroying the fish and all life-forms within the water. They are also causing a great disturbance within the very core of your planet, resulting in greater and greater energy being built within and around the planet. This greater energy is stimulating the negative emotions within the human being. So with this stimulation there is greater desire for control, for power.

My people are monitoring the situation, as they are

monitoring all aggression that is occurring within certain areas of your world. My people are trying to impress upon you the need for the light of love to be brought around your world, so defusing a very volatile situation. In certain areas there is light penetrating through to your people. In other areas there is the density of negative emotion, so darkness envelops these areas.

There is a need for your people to become aware of the futility of aggression, of the futility of destruction. I use 'futility', particularly, because there is no 'death'. There is eternal life. So, in causing 'death', they are in fact stimulating the eternal life within the individual. In doing so, they are instilling into this individual great regret, great pain through the memories of their early transition from the World of Matter to the World of Light. All that occurs to you does not belong to your vehicle, it belongs to the Spirit. It is the Spirit that will continue, and many have difficulty, when coming to my world, releasing the hatred within them. This results in a weakness of the Spirit, causing a slowing down of eternal progress.

My people now come to the people of your world, to try and bring the knowledge that it is futile to cause destruction. It is of great benefit to build and not to remove. Begin to build the light around yourselves, then those who come to you will see and will feel this energy and they will desire to learn. You will then be able to transmit the information. Very slowly an arc of light will built around your world, and within this light my people will be able to descend and bring to you the visions of the future.

To assist your world, it is important for you to concentrate your thoughts upon, and encircle your world with the power of the 'white' light. Within the centre of this power visualise the 'blue' light, to provide an energy that will result in a balancing taking place. A healing of all that exists will then occur, so allowing this build of energy to subside to a relatively peaceful degree. Only then will a true movement take place, one that will encompass all Spirit.

The attempt, by your planet, to move is resulting in certain other forms of Spirit being left behind. It is because of the increase in energy within the very core of your planet that a build of energy is now taking place. Your people know that this build of energy is beginning to manifest in many areas. Your world is trying to go forwards. Many of your people are trying to hold back, because when the transition eventually arrives, the life existence of all 'beings' will alter. Your people prefer to gain wealth, so there is a great disturbance and a rise and manifestation of the physical energies associated with the World of Matter. This is resulting in greater aggression, anger, greed and jealousy, and a rise in the demand for control and power. So there is a great disturbance being shown to many of you.

To alleviate this problem, there is a surge of energy being directed from the World of Light to your planet; an energy that is, as I have already spoken of, being arched around your world and seen by many, who have a sensitivity, as colour, a colour of healing power. There are many souls in my world who sit to transmit this arc of energy, so making effort to calm the agitated energy of your planet and your people. Now is the time for your people to come together, to consolidate their efforts to match my people, to place their thoughts and energy into transmitting the healing power around your world.

Many groups around your world are gathering together now. They sit to direct the energy of healing, but many direct this healing power to human beings when there is need to direct this power to all life. Your World of Matter was designed, was created for all life-forms. All 'life' deserves the right to reside in the 'schoolroom of learning' and to travel along 'their' chosen pathway, without another 'being' deciding for themselves, to prematurely terminate that pathway.

There are people, we know, who are striving to alter the energy structure of your world, but there is now a need for greater and greater amounts of people to participate in this transition. The human beings will move with the planet. Those who drag their feet will find difficulty. It is important that the process is speeded up to a considerable degree, because there are changes to take place with your World of Matter and your people need to be prepared.

Gather together in groups. Concentrate your minds upon transmitting the power of the 'white' light around your world, encircling your World of Matter. Within the centre of the 'white' light concentrate your minds upon the power of the 'blue' light, so bringing a healing to all beings. When achieved, send your thoughts to the skies, as there are many 'beings', who are a part of your universe, who are part of many universes, who are now gathering around your world. They will not be able to descend at the moment, because your people today do not have tolerance for their fellow human beings, so they will be unable to tolerate another kind, another 'being' not of the human structure. So the help, guidance and information that these 'beings' possess, to aid and assist your transition, is currently being placed in a bank within the World of Light and there are Companions who have access to the bank. They will deliver certain aspects of this information to the people who are open and aware of the existence of the Spirit, the existence of the World of Light. I reassure you all that you have the capability of succeeding. You will succeed. The Great Spirit is giving all of you the love and the power to help you.

Humour assists in increasing the energy. Many of your people have great tears, great heartache, pain and suffering. We are very aware of this and many times I stand by and cry for your people. I and my people try to make you aware of our presence, but, because of indoctrination over many, many years, your people turn away, and so we cry, because we cannot help. All we are able to do is to send our love to encircle these people, to try and assist in lightening the energy.

The best form of healing for all life is the concentration of the power of your mind, the power of the Spirit, upon increasing the energy that is refined, around your world. Those who come under the umbrella of this energy will gain healing, an inner peace from the centre of their being. This begins the healing that will take the 'being' away from their suffering. Many of your medical men and women always attack the outside. How many go within? Always consider the Spirit. Consider the mind. Consider the 'Whole'. A finer and finer vibration of energy will release many, negative energies that are within and around the Spirit. Many people forget that the negative aspects of the energy have ill effects upon the 'Being', and I talk of the 'Being' because I also refer to the animals, to nature, to the birds in the sky and to fish. All are 'Spirit'. All are 'life'. All are 'energy'.

You now have a pathway to tread, to aid and assist the World of Light and, in so doing, to aid and assist your own growth and development. When the time arrives for you to become a part of the 'Whole', then your progression will benefit the 'Whole'. Do not allow the human overcoat to divert your attention. Many will come around you who will try to persuade you away from your pathway, away from your knowledge. Be strong and have courage. My people transmit to you their strength and courage to add to your own, so giving you power. Allow this power to flow. Allow it to build around you, and, when people come to you, they will see your tranquillity and feel your peace. They will then enquire and you can talk.

CHAPTER 11

Your Destiny Fulfilled

There are many times in your life when you may believe that you have arrived in the wrong place. Wondering why you are here. Wondering, sometimes, whether or not you have made the wrong turn in life. You believe that there are no openings for you, no doorways through which you are able to walk, in order for you to progress within your life. As a result of this uncertainty, you stand still for a period of time. A mist may develop around you, so that you begin to lose some of your vision, some of your control over life. This can be very, very frightening for some people: the movement away from a stable occupation, a stable home, a stable family environment, a stable physical disposition. All of these can create, for you, fear and an inability to formulate your direction in life.

You may feel rejected. You may feel alone, with very little worth. This, within you, will result in stress of the mind, of the body and of the Spirit. You may feel unbalanced, so the emotions begin to rise within you; the anger and the fear, as I have already mentioned. Tears may flow. Words may be spoken in haste. Around you people are beginning to feel the results of your current position. Some may try to help you but others may turn away, because of the human emotion that builds within you. You may feel betrayed and you may wish to withdraw. All motivation begins to seep away and you begin to move within yourself.

This is all part of the human experience. This is all part of the growth and development that comes around you in this lifetime. There are many stages through life. There is the time when you can skip through life with joviality in your heart and the mind of the child. In front of you is a world to be explored, for you to open your arms and take hold and make an impression and grow within your material environment. You may feel you can reach the top of the world, and you may make every effort to do so with the vibrancy of the red energy of power and strength within your field of energy. This is the colour of the child, and the word 'child' is used with great respect. This is an important time for all people in your world. It is needed by you, and it is there in order for you to begin to build within the Spirit.

So time quickly rolls along. Not a moment to spare. Rushing here, rushing there. Here, there, everywhere. No time to sit, no time to contemplate. You are building your empire. You are building your life. Slowly, there will be changes within and around you. As the years go by, the green energy will begin to feed within your field of energy. It will grow. It will deepen and it will begin to radiate within and around you, so you begin to slow down. There will come the yellow of information, of knowledge. There will come, also, the blue of thought around these colours. Slowly, they will mix, they will change and transform, creating all of the hues, all of the depths, all of the light and dark that comes with this mixing process, and you will begin to move in your life. Your pathway will no longer be straight and direct, because these colours will have an effect upon your mind, upon your body and the Spirit. Your considerations, your contemplation, your decisions in life will affect these colours. They will deepen and lighten according to you, according to your view.

Many will storm through life, and then they will reach a wall and be suddenly stopped. This will create a great disturbance within these colours. Others will move more slowly and the changes will be more subtle, more gentle. Nevertheless, there will be change.

As the green begins to penetrate, so the Spirit will begin to come forwards. There will be influences upon the physical, from the Spirit. Some will be aware, others will not, but, nevertheless, it will be there. The Spirit within will begin to talk and will begin to move you. As you begin to work more with the Spirit within, as you begin to allow the green to slow you down, to allow yourself the time to sit and contemplate, so the Spirit within will radiate outwards and around you. As you begin to achieve this movement, many, many Companions from the World of Light will begin to influence you more and more within your life. Their energy will merge with the energy of 'You' the Spirit. The more 'You' allow this energy to expand, the greater the influence that will come to you from the World of Light. The Masters of the Light will bring you knowledge and teachings. They will bring you information that will very slowly transform you, the individual.

Then there comes a time when it is needed for you to turn in your life. You will need to turn a corner. As you know, with all corners, there is a point where the vision is lost. As you move into the bend, you will be unable to see either in front of you or behind you. The straightness of the pathway will be further ahead and further behind. So you are at a point where you cannot see, where the clouds of uncertainty come upon you. At this time, the Companions, the Masters from the World of Light, will be very, very gently guiding you upon this pathway. There may be the need for you to turn more than one corner before you can then see the light shining in front of you; the light that will say to you, "Come this way, this is the direction that is your destiny." In the turning of your corner there will be, as I have said, tears, anger, frustration and impatience. At this time, my colleagues from the World of Light will be standing upon your shoulder. They will be guiding you with a hand that will be placed upon your hand. They can see. They have the vision. They have the foresight, the knowledge to make sure you are moved with gentleness and love towards the right pathway for you, the individual.

Many human beings may seek advice and guidance from other human beings around them. The advice may misdirect some people, because those around you cannot see your destiny. They do not know your pathway, they only know their own pathway. The Companions from the World of Light are with you for the period of time that you are upon this World of Matter, for the period of time that you inhabit the 'schoolroom of life'. They know. They see your pathway. They will know your destiny in five years, in ten years, in twenty years. They will know every pebble upon your path, every boulder that is in front of you and, more importantly, they will know the very important contingency plans when you walk one way and they need you to walk another way. They will allow you to walk a little way, because that walk will provide for you an experience. They will not then run to you and say "Go this way." Very, very gently, they will slowly turn you. It may take a day, it may take a month, it may take a year, it may take ten years, but they will eventually move you to the correct direction and pathway that will lead you to your destiny. During this time there will be many people whom you will meet and greet. There will be many experiences that will go into your whole being and penetrate the mind, the body and the Spirit.

At the end of your journey, you will have within you many jewels of experience, many diamonds, pearls, rubies, and sapphires. All different shapes and colours, but all of them will be very, very valuable. They will be with 'You' the Spirit; not the human being, but the Spirit, for eternity. They will help you to grow as a spiritual being, as a being of light and love. All experiences, whether they are good or bad for you, will be jewels.

The experiences that are necessary for you will always be

placed before you. This is why human beings, animals and all of nature come up against many obstacles during their time in the World of Matter. If you are able to foresee a difficulty that you do not wish to encounter, but which is important to your growth and development, then the Companion beside you will guide you towards the experience. Very often, you will not consciously know that it is of benefit to you, because you will be looking at the situation with your physical eyes, and I am referring to the benefit of the Spirit. Your lifetime here is not of benefit to the physical, it is of benefit to the Spirit, because it is the Spirit that will continue. The physical vehicle that you all now see is merely the vehicle for the Spirit. It is only suitable for the World of Matter. The vehicle is like your overcoat. You will place it around your shoulders for only a period of time. When you no longer require the overcoat, then you will remove the coat from your shoulders and you will continue to walk your pathway.

So when you return to the World of Light, you will then fully appreciate the experience that you may not appreciate now, whilst you are within the very cumbersome environment of the overcoat. You bring with you the jewels of the Spirit. These jewels are obtained by service, by sacrifice of yourself for the comfort of others.

When the termination of physical life occurs, there will be knowledge, within my world, of your transition, and those who have retained the bond of love will gather around you. They will give their help to 'You' the Spirit, to accomplish a very smooth transition from this world, through the veil, to the World of Light. They will welcome you in the covering that you will recognise. I'm quite sure that you would be very taken aback to see a bright light, but to see your loved ones would create, for you, great security and comfort, as with all people. So they will cloak themselves in the covering that is recognisable to you. They will remain with you for a certain period, to help you to adjust to your new environment. There is always great celebration in my world, because the period of 'death' to you, is birth to my people. There is a child once again moving into the womb of the Great Mother and Father Spirit.

Pathway to Eternity

When evening shadows fall
And the light begins to fade,
'Tis but a moment for us all
To recall the emblem of our days.

To reach into the corners of our mind
And unwrap the dusty shawl,
From around forgotten memories we find
We call upon our faith, the last bastion of all.

As we begin life's last journey
To a land of mystery and uncertainty,
A light begins to shine
Along the pathway to eternity.

A gathering of family and friends
Who have travelled the pathway to life's end,
Begins to dissolve the bonds of fear and apprehension
Tied around the dying embers of convention.

Allowing a beacon of light to descend,
To shine around the bend
That lies before us, as we whisper 'Auld Lang Syne'
And prepare to cross the threshold of time.

Words by Companion of the Earth.
Through the inspired writings of
Rev. Gayna Hilary Petit-Gittos (Tywane)

EPILOGUE

There have been times when my people, from the World of Light, have made dramatic approaches to your World of Matter. For a time this has been looked at, then, over the years, the memories begin to fade. So now we are approaching you all in a different dimension, because your thinking has changed dimension.

There has been a subtlety within the mind of the human being that is now removed from the boundaries of religion. At the time when we made dramatic entry, there was the religious understanding of all your people. Today, there is the more clinical approach to all that you see and hear, so we approach you with subtlety.

When we come to your world now, we approach people, like yourselves, who are prepared for knowledge. Not all people are at the point where the knowledge will help them, so we come to you and say, "Talk to people." Then around you will come people who are ready for the knowledge. Then you say to them, "Talk to people" and around them will come people who are ready.

I bring to you knowledge of the reality of my world. Many of your people today do not know of my world, they are contained within the darkness of ignorance. To them you are a beaming light of knowledge. You are, each one of you, candles, lighted. You are Spirit that beams light to the dark areas of your world. You will go and shine with the knowledge of the Spirit to those around you. You have the knowledge of the Spirit World, of continued life. You have the knowledge of Life.

I desire to request that you do not retain the information

within you, but go and inform those around you of your knowledge. I come to you as an ambassador for my world. I now desire you to be an ambassador who will spread the knowledge around your country, around the world, so that your people, the human beings of your world, will gain knowledge of the requirement for peace and harmony within your countries.

I now leave you with my eternal possessions. I leave you with my strength and my courage, for you to go forwards into the darkness of learning and progression, and I leave you with my Love!

THE BLUE MOUNTAIN COLLECTION

Also available:

<u>"Masters of the Light"</u>

A guided meditation tape by Blue Mountain
that helps to connect you with the Spirit World

From

The Blue Mountain Trust Ltd
50-52 Jeffcock Road, Bradmore,
Wolverhampton, West Midlands, England WV3 7AA.

Printed in Great Britain
by Amazon